novice to master

novice to master

AN ONGOING

LESSON

IN THE EXTENT

OF MY OWN

STUPIDITY

Soko Morinaga Roshi

TRANSLATED FROM THE JAPANESE
BY BELENDA ATTAWAY YAMAKAWA

WISDOM PUBLICATIONS • BOSTON

Wisdom Publications
199 Elm Street
Somerville, MA 02144 USA
www.wisdompubs.org

Library of Congress Cataloging-in-Publication Data
Morinaga, Soko, 1925–
    Novice to master : an ongoing lesson in the extent of my
own stupidity / Soko Morinaga ; translated from the Japanese
by Belenda Attaway Yamakawa.
      p. cm.
    ISBN 0-86171-319-2 (alk. paper)
    1. Spiritual life—Zen Buddhism. 2. Zen Buddhism—
Doctrines. I. Title.

BQ9288.M67 2002
294.3'444—dc21   2002016776

ISBN 0-86171-319-2

First Edition
07 06 05 04 03 02
6   5   4   3   2   1

Jacket design: Gopa & Ted2 and Josh Bartok
Interior design: Gopa & Ted2
Cover art: "Daruma" (1912) by Nakahara Nantembo
(1839–1925), hanging scroll, ink on paper, from the
Asian Art Museum of San Francisco, The Avery
Brundage Collection, Chong-Moon Lee Center for
Asian Art and Culture.

Wisdom Publications' books are printed on acid-free
paper and meet the guidelines for the permanence and
durability set by the Council of Library Resources.

Printed in Canada.

table of contents

Part II: TRAINING

Part III: MASTER

publisher's acknowledgment

THE Publisher gratefully acknowledges the generous help of the Hershey Family Foundation in sponsoring the production of this book.

acknowledgments

WARM THANKS to my sister, Carolyn Attaway O'Kelly. To Professor Minoru Tada of Otani University. To Josh Bartok at Wisdom Publications.

Morinaga Roshi offered practical advice at a time when I most needed it. I try to follow, with varying degrees of success, his wise council on matters of practice within daily life. The main thing he urged me to do: translate. Thank you, Roshi.

Belenda Attaway Yamakawa

 preface

A WHILE AGO I gave a public lecture at a university. The speaker who preceded me talked for about an hour and a half, running over his allotted time. The break period between our talks was shortened, and I was called to the podium right away. Concerned for the audience, I opened by asking, "Did you all have time to urinate?"

Apparently this was not what the audience had expected to hear. Perhaps they were particularly surprised because the person standing before them, talking about pissing, was a monk. Everyone broke into hearty laughter.

Having started out on this note, I continued to drive home the point. "Pissing is something that no one else can do for you. Only you can piss for yourself." This really broke them up, and they laughed even harder.

But you must realize that to say, "You have to piss for yourself; nobody else can piss for you" is to make an utterly serious statement.

Long ago in China, there was a monk called Ken. During his training years, he practiced in the monastery of Ta-hui, but despite his prodigious efforts, he had not attained enlightenment. One day Ken's master ordered him to carry a letter to the far-off land of Ch'ang-sha. This journey, roundtrip, could easily take half a year. The monk Ken thought, "I don't have forever to stay in this hall practicing! Who's got time to go on an errand like this?" He consulted one of his seniors, the monk Genjoza, about the matter.

Genjoza laughed when he heard Ken's predicament. "Even while traveling you can still practice Zen! In fact, I'll come along with you," he offered, and before long the two monks set out on their journey.

One day while the two were traveling, the younger monk Ken suddenly broke into tears. "I have been practicing for many years, and I still haven't been able to attain anything. Now, here I am roaming around the country on this trip; there's no way I am going to attain enlightenment this way," he lamented.

When he heard this, Genjoza, thrusting all the strength he had into his words, put himself at the junior monk's disposal: "I will take care of anything that I can take care of for you on this trip," he said. "But there are just five things that I cannot do in your place.

"I can't wear clothes for you. I can't eat for you. I can't shit for you. I can't piss for you. And I can't carry your body around and live your life for you."

It is said that upon hearing these words, the monk Ken suddenly awakened from his deluded dream and attained a great enlightenment, a great *satori*.

I hope that as you read this, you will realize that I am not just talking about myself or about something that happened elsewhere. No, it is about your own urgent problems that I speak.

part one

NOVICE

the prospect
of my own death

IF I WERE TO SUM UP the past forty years of my life, the time since I became a monk, I would have to say that it has been an ongoing lesson in the extent of my own stupidity. When I speak of my stupidity, I do not refer to something that is innate, but rather to the false impressions that I have cleverly stockpiled, layer upon layer, in my imagination.

Whenever I travel to foreign countries to speak, I am invariably asked to focus on one central issue: Just what is satori, just what is enlightenment? This thing called satori, however, is a state that one can understand only through experience. It cannot be explained or grasped through words alone.

By way of example, there is a proverb that says, "To have a child is to know the heart of a parent." Regardless of how a parent may demonstrate the parental mind to a child, that child cannot completely understand it. Only when children become parents themselves do they fully know the heart of a parent. Such an understanding can be likened to enlightenment, although enlightenment is far deeper still.

Because no words can truly convey the experience of enlightenment, here I will discuss the essentials for awakening, the essentials of Zen training.

Zen training is not a matter of memorizing the wonderful words found in the sutras and in the records of ancient teachers. Rather, these words must serve as an impetus to crush the false notions of one's imagination. The purpose of practice is not to increase knowledge, but to scrape the scales off the eyes, to pull the plugs out of the ears.

Through practice, one comes to see reality. And although it is said that no medicine can cure folly, whatever prompts one to realize "I was a fool" is, in fact, just such a medicine.

It is also said that good medicine is bitter to the taste, and, sadly enough, the medicine that makes people aware of their own foolishness certainly is acrid. The realization that one has been stupid seems always to be accompanied by so-called trials and tribulations, by setbacks and sorrows. I spent the first half of my own life writhing under the effects of this bitter medicine.

I was born in the town of Uozu in Toyama Prefecture. The fierce heat of World War II found me studying with the faculty of literature, under Japan's old system of education, in Toyama High School. High school students had been granted formal reprieve from military duty until after graduation from university. When the war escalated, however, the order came down that students of letters were to depart for the front. Presumably, students of science would go on to pursue courses of study in medicine or the natural sciences and thereby provide constructive cooperation in the war effort; students of literature, on the other hand, would merely read books, design arguments, and generally agitate the national spirit.

At any rate, literature students, who came to be treated as nonstudents, had to take the physical examination for conscription at age twenty and were marched, with no exceptions, into the armed forces. What is more, the draft age was lowered by one year, and as if under hot pursuit, at nineteen I was jerked unceremoniously into the army.

We all know that we will die sooner or later. Death may come tomorrow, or it may come twenty or thirty years hence. Only our ignorance of just how far down the road death awaits affords us some peace of mind, enables us to go on with our lives. But upon passing the physical examination and waiting for a draft notice that could come any day, I found the prospect of my own death suddenly thrust before my eyes. I felt as though I were moving through a void day by day. Awake and in my sleep, I rehearsed the various ways in which I might die on the battlefield. But even though I found myself in a tumult of thoughts about death, there was no time for me to investigate the matter philosophically or to engage in religious practice.

People who entered the army in those days rushed in headlong, fervently believing that this was a just war, a war of such significance that they could sacrifice their lives without regret. Setting out in this spirit, we were armed with a provisional solution to the problem of death—or at least it was so in my case.

Among human beings, there are those who exploit and those who are exploited. The same holds true for relations among nations and among races. Throughout history, the economically developed countries had held dominion over the underdeveloped nations. Now, at last, Japan was rising to liberate herself from the chains of exploitation! Therefore, this was a righteous fight, a meaningful fight! How could we begrudge our country this one small life, even if that life be smashed to bits? Such reckless rationalization allowed us to shut off our minds.

And so it was that we students set out in planes, armed only with the certainty of death and fuel for a one-way trip, with favorite works of philosophy or maybe a book about Buddha's Pure Land beside the control stick, certain to remain unread. Many lunged headlong at enemy ships; still many others were felled by the crest of a wave or knocked from the air before making that lunge.

Then, on August 15, 1945, came Japan's unconditional surrender. The war that everyone had been led to believe was so right, the war for which we might gladly lay down our one life, was instead revealed, overnight, as a war of aggression, a war of evil—and those responsible for it were to be executed.

nothing
is certain

FOR BETTER OR FOR WORSE, I returned from the army alive. Over a shortwave radio, an item extremely hard to come by in those days, I listened to the fate of the German leaders who had surrendered just a step ahead of the Japanese. When I heard the sentence that was read aloud at the Nuremburg Trials, "Death by hanging," the one word—*hanging*—lodged itself so tenaciously in my ears that I can still hear its echo. And then (perhaps through an American Occupation Forces policy?), a news film was shown. I saw this film at what is now the site of a department store, on the fifth floor of a crumbling cement block building that had only just narrowly escaped demolition in war-ravaged downtown Toyama.

In one scene, a German general was dragged to the top of a high platform and hanged before a great crowd that had assembled in the plaza. In another scene, the Italian leader Mussolini was lynched by a mob and then strung upside down on a wire beside the body of his lover. The film went on to show us how the dead bodies were subsequently dragged through the streets while the people hurled verbal abuses and flung rocks at them.

Wearing cast-off military uniforms, my classmates and I went back to school, one by one. We returned, young men unable to believe in anything and hounded by the question of right and wrong. Although technically classes were resumed, in reality no studying took place. If a teacher walked into the classroom, textbook under his arm, he would be asked to take a seat on the sidelines while members of the group who had just returned from the army took turns at the podium.

"Fortunately or not, we've been repatriated, and we're able to come back to school. But what we thought to be 'right,' turned out overnight to be 'wrong.' We may live another forty or fifty years, but are we ever going to be able to believe in anything again—in a 'right' that can't be altered, in a 'wrong' that isn't going to change on us? If we don't resolve this for ourselves, no amount of study is ever going to help us build conviction in anything. Well, what do you fellows think?"

This went on day after day.

It so happened that in those days we had a philosophy teacher named Tasuku Hara. He later went on to become a professor in the philosophy department at Tokyo University. He was an excellent teacher, and I was sorry to hear that he died quite young. Anyway, one day this Professor Hara, who was like an older brother to us, stood up and insisted that we let him get a word in.

Taking the rostrum, he proceeded to talk to us, "Kant, the German philosopher in whose study I specialized, said this: We humans can spend our whole lives pondering the meaning of 'good' and 'evil,' but we will never be able to figure it out. The only thing that human beings can do is come up with a yardstick by which to measure good and evil."

"Looking at it this way," he continued, "if we use the yardstick of the Japanese, this war was a holy war, while by American criteria, it was a war of aggression. So your life's work is not to label this 'good' and that 'bad,' but to search for as useful a standard as you can find to apply anywhere you go on this earth. But this grand yardstick is not something you are going to come by in a day. Each of you will have to transcend time and place to find a standard that can have meaning to as many people as possible. And in order to do this, I suggest, first off, that you get on with your high school lessons."

After receiving this most kind and sincere advice, we resumed our classes. We did, however, also continue our self-indulgent theoretical debates. And I, for one, remained in a quandary over this question of good and evil; the problem lodged itself deep in the back of my mind.

I think, in fact, that this was a dilemma of the times for Japan, common not only among young people like us, but among middle-aged and elderly people as well. We had completely lost sight of any ethical norm. I believe Japan had fallen into a state in which people scarcely knew what standards to apply even in raising their own children.

On top of all this, there were major changes in my own private affairs. To begin with, the year before the war ended, I had lost both of my parents in one blow: even as my mother was slipping away, my father suffered a cerebral hemorrhage and died the very next morning, August 24, without having regained consciousness.

I have three older sisters, but all of them had already married and moved away. They were living in Moji, Shanghai, and Manchuria. Travel conditions being what they were in that day, none of my sisters was able to attend the funeral. As the sole survivor on the family registry, I was responsible for the funeral arrangements, which I completed within two days with help from relatives. Then, before I could settle any further affairs, I received my mustering order and found myself off to the army.

Upon my homecoming after the war had ended, I was greeted with the twin problems of property and inheritance taxes. I come from a long line of landowners, and the small amount of land we had was under tenancy in rice fields. My father had always taught me, "There's nothing as dependable as land. Even if there's a fire, it won't burn. If there's a flood, it won't wash away. If a thief sneaks in, he can't cart it off on his back. No matter what else you do in this life, don't you let go of that land!"

It so happened, though, that through no action of my own, my family's land was lost to the government's agrarian reform program. So now with even this gone, what was left to believe in? All that I had ever thought to be certain had turned out to be uncertain.

The war I had thought was holy turned out to be evil. I had not expected my own parents to die so suddenly, and yet there they went, one right after the other. The insurance money that my father had set aside to provide for his children in the event that something should happen to him was subject to a freezing of funds, and not a cent was available for my use. And our ever-dependable land was now lost.

At the same time, prices were constantly on the rise. What could be bought for one yen one day cost ten yen the next, and before one knew it, a one-hundred-yen note was needed! It was practically unheard of in that time for students to hold part-time jobs. Consequently, I hadn't the slightest experience in using these hands and this body to

the encounter at misery's end

So it was, through these mysterious causes and conditions, that I was led to knock at the gates of Zen temples. I still feel very grateful that, after calling at two or three temples, I was brought to Daishuin in Kyoto, where I still reside, to train under Zuigan Goto Roshi. Zuigan Roshi, formerly the abbot of Myoshinji and at that time the abbot of Daitokuji, was a truly great man.

I showed up at Roshi's door with long, stringy hair, unkempt, with a towel hanging from my waist and heavy clogs on my feet. This great man's first words to me were, "Why have you come here?"

In reply, I rambled on for about an hour and a half, covering the particulars of my situation up to and including my present state. Roshi listened in silence, not attempting to insert so much as a single word.

When I had finished my exposition, he spoke, "Listening to you now, I can see that you've reached a point where there's nothing you can believe in. But there is no such thing as practice without believing in your teacher. Can you believe in me?

"If you can, I'll take you on right now, as you are. But if

you can't believe in me, then your being here is just a waste of time, and you can go right on back where you came from."

Zuigan Roshi, for his part, set forth in no uncertain terms from the very beginning the precept of believing wholeheartedly in one's teacher, but I was not sensible enough at that time to yield with a ready and honest "Okay!"

Roshi was then seventy years old, and I told myself, "That foolish old man! So what if he is the head of Myoshinji or the head of Daitokuji. Lots of "important" people in this world aren't worth much. If believing were so easy that I could just believe, unconditionally, in somebody I had just met for the first time, then wouldn't I have believed in something before I ever showed up here? Didn't I come here in the first place because I *don't* find it so easy to believe?"

All this ran through my mind, but I knew from the start that if I said it aloud, I would be told straightaway, "In that case, your being here is a waste of time. Go on home now."

Figuring that, even if my words were a lie, this man would have to let me stay if I spoke them, I said, "I believe in you. Please."

At that time, I had no idea of the weight of those words "I believe," but it was a lesson I was to be taught before the end of that very day.

there is no trash

FOLLOW ME," directed the roshi, and he assigned me my first task, which was to clean the garden. Together with this seventy-year-old roshi, I went out to the garden and started sweeping with a bamboo broom. Zen temple gardens are carefully designed with trees planted to ensure that leaves will fall throughout the entire year. Not only the maples in autumn but also the oaks and the camphors in spring regularly shed their foliage. When I first arrived, in April, the garden was full of fallen leaves.

The human being (or, my own mind, I should say) is really quite mean. Here I was, inside my heart denouncing this "old fool" and balking at the very idea of trusting so easily; yet, at the same time, I wanted this old man to notice me, and so I took up that broom and swept with a vengeance. Quite soon I had amassed a mountain of dead leaves. Eager to show off my diligence, I asked, "Roshi, where should I throw this trash?"

The words were barely out of my mouth when he thundered back at me, "There is no trash!"

"No trash, but...look here, " I tried to indicate the pile of leaves.

"So you don't believe me! Is that it?"

"It's only that, well, where should I throw out these leaves?" That was all that was left for me to say.

"You don't throw them out!" he roared again.

"What should I do then?" I asked.

"Go out to the shed and bring back an empty charcoal sack," was his instruction.

When I returned, I found Roshi bent to the task of combing through the mountain of leaves, sifting so that the lighter leaves came out on top while the heavier sand and stones fell to the bottom. He then proceeded to stuff the leaves into the sack I had brought from the shed, tamping them down with his feet. After he had jammed the last leaves tightly into the sack, he said, "Take these to the shed. We'll use them to make a fire under the bath."

As I went off to the shed, I silently admitted that this sack of leaves over my shoulder was perhaps not trash; I also told myself that what was left of that pile out there in the garden was clearly trash, and nothing but trash. I got back, though, only to find Roshi squatting over the remains of the leaf pile, picking out the stones. After he had carefully picked out the last stone, he ordered, "Take these out and arrange them under the rain gutters."

When I had set out the stones, together with the gravel that was already there, and filled in the spaces pummeled out by the raindrops, I found that not only were the holes filled but that my work looked rather elegant. I had to allow that these stones, too, failed to fall into the category of trash. There was still more, though: the clods of earth and scraps of moss, the last dregs. Just what could anyone possibly do with that stuff, I wondered.

I saw Roshi going about his business, gathering up these scraps and placing them, piece by piece, in the palm of his hand. He scanned the ground for dents and sinks; he filled them in with the clods of earth, which he then tamped down with his feet. Not a single particle remained of the mountain of leaves.

"Well?" he queried, "Do you understand a little bit better now? From the first, in people and in things, there is no such thing as trash."

This was the first sermon I ever heard from Zuigan Roshi. Although it did make an impression on me, unfortunately, I was not keen enough to attain satori as a result of simply hearing these words.

From the first, in people and in things, there is no such thing as trash. These words point to the fundamental truth of Buddhism, a truth I could not as yet conceive in those days.

"Wonder of wonders! Intrinsically all living beings are buddhas, endowed with wisdom and virtue. Only because they cling to their delusive thinking do they fail to realize this." This was Shakyamuni Buddha's exclamation at the instant of his enlightenment. To put it in other words, all beings are, from the first, absolutely perfect, but because people are attached to deluded notions, they cannot perceive this innate buddha-nature.

In the classical Chinese sutras it is written that Shakyamuni said, "I attained buddhahood together with all the grasses, the trees, and the great earth."

In a split second, the mist before his eyes cleared, and Shakyamuni Buddha could see the true form of reality. "Up to now, I thought all beings in this world were living only in pain and misery, in deep unhappiness. But, in reality, aren't all beings, just as they are, living in buddhahood, living in a state of absolute perfection? And doesn't this apply not only to those who are healthy and sound of body, but also to those who are blind, to those without hands, to the ones who are barely dragging themselves along? Isn't each and every one, just exactly as he or she presently is, a perfect and flawless being?" Awed and astonished, the Buddha called out in the voice of satori.

Every year, I go to Hokkaido to lecture, and one year, there was a woman present who asked to meet me after the talk. The young woman, an ardent believer in Christianity, had this to say: "Listening to your talk today, I could see that about all Buddhism tells us to do is throw away our desires. On the other hand, Christianity says, 'Ask, and it shall be given you. Seek, and you shall find. Knock, and the door shall be opened to you.' This teaching answers the hopes of young people like myself. What do you think about this, Roshi?"

I answered her with a question of my own. "Is that to say that no matter how you knock, no matter how you seek, you shall receive, and the door will be opened to you? Is it not the case that unless one knocks and seeks in a way that is in accord with the heart of God, the door surely will not be opened, nor will one's desires be granted?"

I have heard the Christian teaching, "You devise your way, but God directs your steps." In sum, you desire and choose and seek as you please, but it is God who decides whether or not your wishes are to be granted.

So, too, Buddhism does not say only to throw away all desire, to toss aside all seeking. It is especially in the Zen sect that we seek, that we knock at that door through a practice so intensive as to be like carving up our very bones. Buddhism points out, however, that after all the seeking, what we attain is the realization that what we have sought was always, from the beginning, already ours; after all the pounding away, we awaken to the fact that the door was already open before we ever began to knock.

So you see, Zuigan Roshi pointed out the most basic truth right from the start when he said, "From the first, in people and in things, there is no such thing as trash." Unfortunately, I did not understand him. I went on pretending to be a disciple who trusts his roshi, while inside my heart I criticized and resisted. To tell you the truth, I found almost everything he said irritating.

consumed
with cleaning

M ANY PEOPLE look down on activity that pertains to the basic necessities, but I myself do not regard such work as menial. If you desire to gaze out over wide vistas, you do well to climb up to a high spot. But if you wish to gaze into the human heart, you must climb down and look from a low place.

As soon as I entered a Zen temple, I was made to do just that through a routine of all-out cleaning. From morning to night, my mind came to be consumed with cleaning. This led to quite a preposterous experience, and one that illustrates a thorny aspect of practice.

If a person knows that they can come to some understanding of truth through the practice of cleaning, they just may get caught up in the practice and find that they are actually moving further away from seeing truth. Their own heart has become fettered by that practice.

One morning, after I had prepared the meal and given the call to breakfast, Zuigan Roshi slowly entered the dining room and said, "Hey, go into my room and, from my desk, look toward the alcove."

Generally, to the ears of a novice monk, the Zen master's

manner of speaking comes across much like anger. So when I heard Roshi's words, I thought with a start, "Uh-oh, I bungled the cleaning again!" and immediately rushed to his room.

Roshi's room was small, four and a half tatami mats. The distance between his desk and the alcove could not have measured two meters, but though I carefully inspected the area, I could not find even so much as as a bit of dust or a drop of water left from the swab. I crawled about the room on all fours, but I could not find a problem anywhere.

I planted myself there for a while and tried to think it out, but I hadn't a clue as to why Roshi was irritated with me. It couldn't be helped; I resigned myself to being yelled at again and returned to the dining room. "I don't understand what I did wrong in the cleaning," I nervously admitted to Roshi. "Please show me."

"You fool!" he came back at me. "Who said you did anything wrong in the cleaning? This morning I put that single rose of Sharon in the bud vase. It goes well with the scroll and looks so beautiful, so I told you to go look at it. You did see the flower, didn't you?"

It dawned on me that I had not, in fact, noticed a flower. I went back into Roshi's room to look. The wall of the alcove, which had been standing for over 250 years, was darkened. Against the smoky wall there was a scroll with the single large calligraphy of the ideograph for *dew*.

When a Zen monk writes the word *dew*, it is not to the natural phenomenon that he refers, but to direct revelation. Nothing concealed anywhere. Truth, or Dharma, revealed in all things. Buddha revealed in all things. If you all just let the scales drop from your eyes, you realize then that everything everywhere is filled with truth; everything everywhere is filled with Buddha; everything everywhere is to be appreciated! This is what the scroll of *dew* was hanging there to say.

Beneath the scroll, a large pure white blossom seemed to float out from the old plastered wall and bathe the eye with its beauty.

Just moments before, I had failed to see that flower. My eyes had been tightly shut to it. Herein lies the difficulty of practice.

My oversight was to become grist for my teacher's lectures. After I made this blunder, Zuigan Roshi was wont to say during talks, "If the heart is caught up, fettered, you cannot see even what you are looking right at. Why, just the other day, that idiot who is sitting right over there...."

confucius gives jan yu a scolding

THE SEVENTY-ONE-YEAR-OLD roshi who took me in as his disciple had worked hard at Tokyo University and graduated at the top of his class; he had seen his way through Zen training and had served as the head of the Daitokuji temple complex. Such was his personal history, and here I was—twenty or thereabouts, with nothing to offer but a high school education under the old system, no university training—becoming his disciple. From my own lowly state, I looked up to Roshi as one would look up to the Himalayas.

So there I was, in the early days of practice, already despairing of my future, as if there were really no use going on, torturing myself with the notion that there was just no way I would ever be fit to walk in Roshi's footsteps. Every now and again, sensing some indication of praise from Roshi, I would soar to the heavens, but I would promptly drive myself back down to the bottoms of despair.

My dilemma was not unique. Perhaps most everyone, from times of old to today, who has set out to practice has suffered the same problem. There was Tzu-lu, for instance, a disciple of Confucius' in ancient China. Tzu-lu had lived a hooligan's life until the day he unceremoniously barged into the place where Confucius was quietly teaching the Way of the Saints. Struck with the master's character, Tzu-lu became his disciple. This Tzu-lu was a man who had complete confidence in his own physical strength, but he quickly realized that Confucius was not only a man who taught the Way of Virtue through his own gentle and virtuous character but that he also possessed a strength that Tzu-lu could not begin to match. Confucius had a profound understanding of the psychology of the lower classes that prompted Tzu-lu to wonder what kind of life this man had led in his earlier days. The range and depth of Confucius's knowledge were so vast that his disciples were at a loss to know exactly what to make of him. Though a diligent disciple, Tzu-lu feared he would never match his master.

On another occasion, Confucius was heard praising one of his many disciples, Yen Hui, saying, "That Hui! A single bamboo bowl, a gourdful of drink, living in a back alley. Others would have found such a life unbearably depressing, but Hui's good humor was not dampened a bit. Worthy indeed was Hui!"

Confucius was essentially saying, "Ah, that disciple of mine, Yen Hui, what a great human being he was. He ate the poorest food, drank only water"—in China where the water was bad, having tea to drink was simply taken for granted, so to lead a life where one has only water to drink was quite remarkable!—"and he lived in the slums. Most people would find such a life unendurable and fall into despair. But not Yen Hui! Even in the midst of that life, nothing stopped him from happily following the Way. What a wonderful fellow was Yen Hui!"

Now, Jan Yu, a disciple who was present at the time, raised a concern, "It is not that I do not believe in the wonderful Way, which you, my master, and my excellent seniors such as Yen Hui have practiced. It is only that some of us lack the power to practice that way."

Confucius, quite out of character, sprang upon Jan Yu in forceful rebuke for his self-indulgence, "Lack of ability is an excuse for those who have at least tried, at least come partway. But you! Before even setting out to try anything, you set limits on your ability."

Confucius gave Jan Yu a sound scolding.

Everyone will have times when they may want to utter such refrains, trying to escape responsibility. Even I, speaking as I do now about Jan Yu's scolding, was once a disciple who felt exactly as he did. "There's just no way. Roshi could do it because he understands Buddhism, and he is a great human being. But me, I am just an ordinary person and, well..." This is not humility; it is nothing more than self-cherishing self-defense!

And now I recognize what kind of image my own disciples have of me. While they may not look up to me quite as highly as I looked up to Zuigan Roshi, they still seem to imagine that it is beyond their power to equal me.

That being the case, just what is it that I have accomplished up to now? I was not inspired to work my way into and out of Tokyo University as did Zuigan Roshi. Neither have I become a chief abbot. What I have done is only this: When it has been my turn to work in the kitchen, I have given everything I've got to working in the kitchen.

There is no way you can exert yourself in this world without that exertion being of value. Each and every thing is the form that the heart is presently taking, the revelation of Buddha, a manifestation of Dharma. When I first entered the monastery, Zuigan Roshi, sweeping beside me in the garden, called this fact to my attention when he said, "Well, do you get it? From the first, in people and in things, there is no trash." I surely took the far and round-about way of coming to understand this in terms of actual practice, though.

"Meeting with a broom, become that broom; meeting with a bowl of rice, become that bowl of rice." Such expressions are standard fare in Zen, but the question is: How do you put it into practice in daily life?

working it out
for myself

IN ZEN TEMPLES, a breakfast of rice porridge is followed by tea in the roshi's room. The roshi goes over the day's schedule while a bowl of powdered green tea is whisked and served, first to him and then to the others. When I first went to train under Zuigan Roshi, a certain woman, Miss Okamoto, was living at Daishuin. This elderly lady had graduated from Ochanomizu Women's College in the Taisho era and had worked in young women's education for many years in both Tokyo and Kyushu. When she was over forty years old, she became a serious disciple of Roshi. She quit her job and moved to be near her teacher, and, dressed in baggy work pants every day, she helped take care of him until the day he died. At that time, there were only the three of us living there, and during teatime Roshi would talk with Miss Okamoto, but he never deigned to utter a word to me.

One day Miss Okamoto, probably out of pity, sought to bring me into the conversation. "And what do you think, Morinaga?"

"No, no," came Roshi's intervention. "This one is not yet fit to speak in front of anybody."

It was Roshi's view that in order to speak before others, one should thoroughly know oneself. This verifying of one's own essential nature is called *kensho* in Zen. Those who have not had kensho are not considered qualified to speak in front of other people.

This incident irked me, and once again I cursed in silence, "This hateful old man! While he proclaims that nobody and no thing are trash, isn't he treating *me* like trash?"

I thought this to myself. But if I had dared let my attitude show, that would have been it! Roshi would have told me without hesitation, "Well, you can go on home now. There's no practice under a roshi that you can't respect and trust."

From this teatime experience, I understood that true belief is to accept without objections. I must agree to undertake every task, no matter how impossible it may seem. Even if I am told to do three things at once, even if I am told to do something I have never before attempted, I must never, under any circumstances, say, "I can't do it. That's impossible."

What was I to do then? As if for dear life, I had to pour all of my concentrated effort into the task—that is the only way. The very first thing that Zuigan Roshi hammered into me was belief in the teacher. That meant that I had to work things out for myself, through all-out effort, without complaint.

"i can't do it"

WHEN MY PARENTS were alive and well, I grumbled ceaselessly, and the words "I can't do it" were quick to roll off my tongue. I came to notice, however, that this "I can't do it" that I was forever mouthing was not, in reality, an unbiased assessment of an objective impossibility, but only an impossibility based upon my own assessment of my power at that moment.

When you feel you have a capacity of, say, 10.0, anything up to 9.9 feels possible; the feeling "I can't do it" arises just at the point at which you are given a 10.1 assignment. The person who is quick to judge a task as impossible will never perform any task beyond a 10.0. That person will never improve. For this reason, you must never think, "I can't do it."

No matter what demands the teacher makes of you, you must somehow fulfill them. You make unyielding efforts to work it out, and as you climb—10.1, 10.2, 10.3—you gradually develop, for the first time, power you never thought yourself capable of having.

Suppose, now, that my master ordered, "Kill!" or "Die!"

Would I really have to kill, or die? What in the world would I do? Given such orders, how can one continue to believe in one's teacher?

First of all, one realizes that the teacher in whom one believes would never instruct one to do something unethical. It follows, then, that when the teacher uses the words *kill* and *die*, the words have a hidden, deeper meaning, one that the student does not yet understand.

Then, accepting that the words have another, deeper meaning, yet not knowing what that meaning is, the student finds himself or herself assailed by a great doubt. Driven by this doubt, spurred on by the constant sense of a problem, they proceed desperately with concentrated practice. This, in Zen, is "to believe."

Phrases such as "Kill the Buddha, kill the ancestors" and even "Kill your father, kill your mother" show up throughout the writings of the Zen sect. "Belief" in Zen is working through, in practice, exactly what on earth this all means. Regardless of what one is told, regardless of the task assigned, one tenaciously carries it through, without complaint. This diligence characterized the first stage of my life as a novice monk.

This is not to say, though, that I performed all my assignments creditably or even competently. For example, there was the time, on my first day, when I was told to wipe the floors. I sat down on my knees on the wood floor with my legs folded under me and proceeded to wipe from right to left, holding the rag in one hand. However, the wooden floors of a Zen temple are far more vast than those of any ordinary house.

"You fool! How many days do you plan to spend wiping that floor? *This* is the way you wipe a floor." When I saw

Roshi down on all fours, his bottom up in the air, pressing the rag to the floor with both hands, and running swiftly up and down the corridor, I felt as if the scales obscuring my vision were dropping from my eyes.

In the literature department in high school, my classmates and I had read philosophy and ushered in many a new dawn debating with each other. Talk about theorizing! I had put in my time at that particular activity long before I reached the temple. But that was all talk, and in reality, I could not even wipe the floor properly, could I? I felt terribly ashamed of myself when I realized this. I decided then that I would try to do my very best. But I still did not know toward what, exactly, I should direct my energy.

During the day a group of young people would come to the temple from the outside. If one of them took a bamboo broom and commenced to sweep the garden, I would swoop down on him, announcing, "Here, I'll do that!"—and grab the broom out of his hands. If another started to wipe the floor, I would soon be down on her, grabbing the rag, "Here, I'll do that!" If another started to make a fire under the bath, I would fly in to take over the job, declaring, "Here, I'll do that!"

Finally, I had them all shouting at me, *"Can't you find a job without grabbing somebody else's?"*

I could not, for the life of me, understand just what I was doing wrong. That is because I could not work things out for myself, through my own efforts.

Now, when students come to my temple to do zazen, the first job I give them is to make the bath. Bearing in mind that students occasionally light fires under empty baths, I initially probe them with a few questions.

"You are going to make the bath. What is the first thing you do?"

Likely as not, the answer comes, "Light the fire."

"You're going to do that to me, are you?" I ask.

"Oh, no. First I fill the tub with water," says the student.

"You're going to put in water, just like that?" This puzzles them because they have no concept of cleaning the bath first. After covering the basics—clean the bath, fill the tub with water, check the water level, put the lid on, make the fire—I come back to find them beside the fuel feed hole, looking perplexed. Peeking inside, I see a couple of fat logs perched atop some newspaper cinders.

"That's not going to catch on fire, is it? Hadn't you better use smaller sticks of wood?" I ask.

"But there aren't any smaller sticks of wood."

'Well, what about splitting some?"

"I don't know where the hatchet is."

"Well, if you don't know where it is, why don't you ask?"

After all this, the young student is set to splitting firewood. But that is not to say that a blazing fire is imminent. Smoke pours from the hole, and the fire refuses to take off. When I come to survey the situation, I see that the ash from the previous fire has not been removed. So I ask, "Hey, what is this thing called a fire anyway?"

"Well, it's the compounding of oxygen and matter."

"Where is the oxygen?"

"It's in the air."

"So why, then, don't you get rid of this ash so that the air can enter freely? And if the chimney is stopped up, you ought to clean that as well."

If I say this, the young student will climb to the roof to clean the chimney, but on their way back down they will, without fail, stomp on and break two or three tiles.

But I cannot laugh at young people like this because I was exactly like them at one time!

between teacher
and student

ONE MORNING during the novice period of my training, Miss Okamoto asked Zuigan Roshi the following question during teatime: "Roshi, who was greater, Kosen Roshi or Soen Roshi?"

Some background information is needed here. I will give it in the form of a chart.

```
                    Kosen
                      |
                    Soen
             ┌────────┴────────┐
         Sokatsu            Josho
            |
         Zuigan
            |
          Sesso
            |
           Soko
```

I am the "Soko" who appears last on the list, and Sesso is my elder brother in the Dharma. We both had Zuigan

Roshi for our master, and his master was Sokatsu Roshi. If you trace the line all the way back, you arrive at Shakyamuni Buddha.

In the Zen school, the lineage of those great monks who have carried through with their training to attain satori is clearly known. This religious experience must be certified by the master, and only those who receive the seal of transmission of the Dharma enter into the lineage. We know exactly who has received the seal from which master, and these successions are carefully preserved. In the Rinzai sect, the honorific title "Roshi" is used to refer to persons within these lines.

Kosen Roshi, who appears on the lineage chart above, refers to Kosen Imakita, an outstanding master who was the abbot of Engakuji in Kamakura from the latter days of the Tokugawa Period into the Meiji Period in the nineteenth century. During the time of the persecution of Buddhists, he rose above sectarianism and spared no efforts to revive Buddhism. There is a book about him by the lay man D. T. Suzuki, who greatly admired him.

Kosen Roshi's Dharma successor, Soen Shaku Roshi, who was the first to propagate Zen in America, also served as abbot of Engakuji in Kamakura. Soseki Natsume was one of the many who practiced Zen under this roshi.

It was these two men to whom Miss Okamoto referred when she asked who was greater.

Zuigan Roshi, very austere and not one to joke, answered with a solemn face, "The master Kosen was greater."

"Well, then, of Soen Roshi and Sokatsu Roshi, who was greater?" continued Miss Okamoto.

The Sokatsu Roshi to whom she now referred was one who chose not to live in a famous temple after he received the Dharma sanction to teach, but, instead, connected himself with a tiny hermitage called Ryoboan, in the Yanaka district of Tokyo, where he worked with lay householders in Zen practice. The first women to become famous for their outspoken stance on women's rights in Japan were among his many followers. This Sokatsu Roshi was one of the subjects in question, but Zuigan Roshi replied, "The master Soen was greater."

"Oh, Roshi, that's terrible! Isn't the lineage gradually thinning down to nothing? Well, who is greater, Sokatsu Roshi or Zuigan Roshi?" Miss Okamoto persisted.

Zuigan Roshi, responding to the lady's concern that the lineage was thinning down to nothing, promptly answered, "I'm greater."

Up to this point, it had always been the master who had been greater. But now when he comes to his own place in line he says, "I am greater than my teacher."

This thoroughly pleased Miss Okamoto, who then asked, "Well, in that case, Roshi, who is greater, you or your disciple, Mr. Sesso?"

At this, I thought I would burst out laughing. Zuigan Roshi, who had already filled the posts of abbot of Myoshinji and Daitokuji, was a high peak in the Zen world. His disciple, Mr. Sesso, who did not even have his own temple yet, was living as a mere caretaker in a small hermitage inside the Myoshinji complex, just keeping the garden clean. Because I did not as yet have any insight into human beings' intrinsic qualities and could only judge in terms of their social positions, I thought that comparing Zuigan Roshi and Mr. Sesso was like comparing the moon and a turtle. There was simply no contest, and I was right on the verge of laughing out loud.

Zuigan Roshi, without stopping for even a second to consider, said, "Well, we don't know that yet."

When these words hit me, my face, which had been ready to burst into laughter, immediately straightened, and now, in spite of myself, I thought I was going to cry. I felt so blessed to be with this teacher. He might scold me unmercifully, call me worthless, and say that I am not fit to talk in front of anybody, but he always has his eye out to the future of his disciples. I realized that, even faced with my present immaturity, he believed in what I could become in a year, in two years, ten years, twenty years. Always bearing in mind my potential future form as well as my present one, he worked with me. I could feel this come through strongly when he said, "Well, we don't know that yet."

As it turns out, this Mr. Sesso managed, some years later, to live up to these words, becoming the successor of Zuigan Roshi and then the abbot of Daitokuji. Following the instructions of Zuigan Roshi, I was able to stay by Sesso Roshi's side for many years, and I later became his Dharma successor. At the time of his death, Sesso Roshi had achieved a towering state of mind, not inferior to that of his own teacher.

So, that single episode that one morning at teatime enabled me, at last, to trust my teacher from the bottom of my heart.

But even so, I still did not seem to get anywhere in my practice.

that's between
him and me

ONE MORE ANECDOTE will further illustrate trust
between teacher and student. Soen Roshi had
a disciple named Josho Ota. This disciple later went on to
become the abbot of Engakuji and then to serve as abbot
of Daitokuji, but the incident I will relate occurred when
he was still in training under Soen Roshi.

One summer day, a devotee came to Engakuji with an
invitation for Soen Roshi saying, "Roshi, here at the temple
you always eat what the monks prepare, but on this hot
summer day, I would like to treat you to dinner, a small
offering that may help you to forget the heat."

"So, there's going to be a feast, eh?" replied Soen Roshi,
who was a very easygoing man. He gathered up his disciple,
Josho, and set out for the restaurant.

As it was summertime, the bamboo doors separating the
individual tatami rooms were left open, permitting guests
to see directly into the rooms surrounding their own. Soen
Roshi heartily ate and drank his fill and became altogether
jolly. He picked up slices of the raw fish and remarked,
"Ah, what rare vegetables! Why don't the monks grow
these in our garden?" and generally carried on in this way

until he was finally, in fact, down to his loincloth, dancing a naked jig.

The roshi was quite famous, his name known even abroad. Soon there was a ripple moving through the guests in adjacent rooms, "Isn't that the abbot of Engakuji dancing naked over there?" Josho slipped over and shut the bamboo doors.

Without warning, the roshi seized Josho by the collar and began to scold him, saying, "Hey! Are you criticizing my behavior? Did you shut that door because you think I'm doing something wrong?"

Josho, who had shown a lapse of confidence in his teacher, suddenly found himself being showered with blows.

Zen monks undergo a training that is founded more on actions than on words. But even allowing for that, considerable saké had flowed into this particular situation, and the end did not appear to be in sight even after the roshi had administered five and six blows. Josho, who had silently and obediently endured the first thrusts, refused to take more. Seizing his teacher's hands, he spoke up, "Roshi or no roshi, you are not going to get away with any more of this."

Soen Roshi shook his hands free and went back to his seat. Looking as though nothing whatsoever had happened, he continued drinking until he returned, in quite high spirits, to Engakuji.

Although the matter was settled right then and there, the devotee who had invited them to dinner felt horribly anxious about the whole affair. Knowing that the master-disciple relationship is very rigid, he worried that the roshi would expel Josho when they returned to the temple. Feeling that he simply could not leave the situation hanging, he soon made his way to Engakuji to act as a mediator.

"Thank you so much for doing me the honor of accepting my poor offering today and for showing pleasure in dining with me," he said to the roshi. "I would also like to add that, although Josho was very discourteous to you at dinner, I am certain he meant no ill will. I beg that you will, for my sake, dismiss the whole affair and forgive him."

"That's between him and me," was the roshi's terse reply.

Please understand that the roshi was not saying here that this was a problem between himself and his disciple and that interference was unwelcome. He was saying that he and his student might trade kicks and blows, but between the two of them, there was not a gap of even a single hair. For a Zen practitioner to have his teacher say this about him is something to be appreciated, but for a teacher to have a disciple who allows it to be said is also a wonderful thing. I have heard, by the way, that the devotee who sought to intervene in the relationship withdrew blushing after he heard this short reply.

This story calls to my mind the relationship between sumo wrestlers and the ring. The reason that two giant men, together weighing in at well over five hundred pounds, can come together and wrestle, slamming all their might into the contest, is that there is a ring under them, which, like the bond between master and disciple, absolutely will not break. If a wrestler, however skillful, were to compete inside a ring drawn on ice, wouldn't he creep around, throwing all his effort instead into ensuring that the ice did not break?

three types
of students

IN ZEN PRACTICE, it is necessary to "break the
ego"—there is no way around it. Furthermore, if
one is timid about breaking this ego—which strenuously
resists being broken—then the case is hopeless. Those
who do not clench their teeth and hang in there, despite
being slapped and kicked, beaten and driven out, will not
hold out in this thing called practice. For this reason, it is
said that disciples fall into three categories, based upon
their relations with their teacher: "The best students are
attached by hatred, the mediocre by charity, and the worst
by authority."

The best is a first-class disciple, or a person of deep
virtue. From the outside, such students might even appear
hostile. The tougher the master treats them, the more
they dig in, resolutely swearing to carry through, to show
the master what they can accomplish. Nothing can make
such students loosen their bite.

Mediocre disciples are those who are really having a
hard time of it and would like to back out, but feel they
cannot possibly quit, what with the roshi bending over

backward to be so kind and supportive. These students are pulled along by the roshi's affection.

Lastly, the inferior students are those who, observing the roshi's secular authority, "seek the shade of a big tree." That is to say, they figure that if they must rely on someone, it had better be someone who appears powerful. This maxim, "Inferior people are attached by authority"—does not stop at the gates of a Zen temple, but holds true for society in general.

All this calls to mind another of my many blunders, one that I made after I'd been practicing for some time. Someone happened to point out one of my shortcomings, and I lit in, "What the hell do you know!" and gave him a thrashing. I was displaying the swollen head that one sometimes suffers partway along in practice, a sort of "rust from training."

When word of this incident reached my teacher, he called me to his room, without delay, to inform me that I was dismissed from the temple. The way he said it was, "Pack your bags."

Pressing my forehead to the floor, I earnestly apologized for over thirty minutes, but my pleas for forgiveness were in vain.

"I didn't think it over deeply and then decide to do it. It just happened by accident, when I was off guard," I offered as an excuse.

"If it were something you decided to do after thinking it over deeply, and if you then noticed that you were in the wrong, it probably would not happen again," he countered, "but if it happened 'by accident' when you were 'off guard,' it arose from someplace deep in your heart, in your disposition. This being the case, forgiving you is all the more unjustified!"

I had exhausted all means of apology. Finally, I raised up this body, which had been flattened out in prostration like a cringing spider, and looked Roshi straight in the face. His eyes had always looked big, but as he brought his gaze to bear upon me then, in a glare, it was as though his whole face had become just those giant eyeballs. I glared back, not giving an inch.

"There is nowhere for me but next to you. You can throw me out a thousand times or ten thousand times, but I absolutely will not leave your side!" I screamed out.

To my surprise, tears welled up in Roshi's eyes, and I thought they were going to roll down his cheeks in big drops. Then I heard him say, "I forgive you. Go on out and get to your work now."

When I remember this, even now, tears come to my own eyes.

The master employs strictness severe enough to arouse even hatred, feeling that the disciple will somehow be able to carry through to the end. No, in fact, the master really administers strictness with a deep prayer that the disciple will be able to carry through. If one of my own disciples today were to tell me, "Even if it kills me, I will never leave your side," I'm sure that I, too, would cry.

So you can see why I feel grateful when I reflect on the way my teacher, who is no longer alive, behaved toward me. He acted, from start to finish, as though I, a real good-for-nothing, were the best type of student. If Roshi had assessed me differently, if he had thought, "If I'm not careful, this one may drop out," he may well have treated me more indulgently.

"for the disposal
of your remains"

I HAVE SHOWN how a fellow, myself, who could not
do anything properly, was taken in hand and
turned into somebody who could at least cook food over a
wood fire, make a bath, clean a toilet, and work in a garden. And, in time, I was also taught other things, such as
sutra reading and the etiquette appropriate for a priest.

And then one day, after I had been at Daishuin over a
year, the roshi said to me, "It is necessary for human
beings, especially those who become priests, to have con-
tact with other people. You must not live in isolation. You
must form plenty of relationships. While it is, in a sense,
sufficient for a disciple to practice alone under one
teacher, for the purpose of forming social ties with others,
you must go to a training hall."

There are two types of Zen temples. Monks generally
live in one type, as novices, until they graduate from the
university. Once graduated, young monks gather in a professional monastery in order to carry on intensive zazen
practice. It was decided that I would enter Daitokuji
monastery for this latter type of training.

A monk takes with him to the professional training hall

a sort of box to carry his robes in. It is traditionally a frugal affair made of thick paper hardened by lacquer, about a size larger than a book satchel. Bowls and chopsticks for eating, razor and sharpening stone for shaving the head, sutra books, underclothes, and a raincoat are packed into two bundles and tied up with string so that the monk can carry all his worldly belongings on his back. He tucks his robes up at the waist, wraps his legs in gaiters, ties up his straw sandals, dons a wicker hat, and sets out for the monastery.

I was preparing my robe box when the roshi came into the room and asked, "How is it going? Have you tied up your box yet?"

"No, not yet. That is what I was just about to do."

"Well, it's good timing then. Bring the lid of your box with you, and come into my room," he instructed.

This box, like a medicine chest, is completely covered by a lid. Wondering what roshi had in mind, I carried the lid into his room. The roshi took the lid from me and pasted three one-thousand-yen notes to its underside. (In those days, a one-thousand-yen note still carried some clout!)

"Do you understand the meaning of this?" questioned the roshi after he had done this.

"Is it pocket money?" I started to ask, but checked myself before the words were out, knowing that I would be yelled at if I said something clumsy.

Roshi was already at the advanced age of seventy-one when I showed up begging to be taken in as his disciple. He had warned me then, "I don't know how much longer I'm going to live. If your teacher dies on you, you might get cut off in the middle of your training. If there is nobody to take care of your financial needs, you are in trouble. You had better look for a younger master."

"I still have something left from my father. I will not be a financial nuisance to you at all," I had pleaded.

With this promise, I had been taken under Roshi's wing as his disciple. In accordance with our agreement, he had never given me a penny for spending money.

Now, I was leaving for the monastery, and I thought that Roshi, even being as steadfast as he is, might be sending me off with some funds for personal expenses. Contrary to my expectations, however, he informed me, "This is nirvana money."

The figure of Shakyamuni Buddha lying on his side to die is known as the "nirvana figure."

"You're heading out now for the training hall where you will lay down your life. If fortune goes against you, you'll fall out and die by the wayside during training. So that you don't become a burden to anybody, this money is for the disposal of your body."

Roshi was ordinarily very stern and did not indulge in jokes. To hear him say, with that solemn face, "This money is for the disposal of your body," sent a shudder down my spine. With renewed determination, I vowed to myself, *"I will do it!"*

I had thought about death before, as a student departing for the war front; however, the death implied in Roshi's words—"This money is for the disposal of your remains"—had a completely different meaning. It was not the death of the physical body to which he referred, but the death of my own ego.

No matter how cleverly we might manipulate ideas, coming right down to it, our real motive is to pamper our own precious selves. Unless we practice to overcome the obstinate attachment to looking out for our own dear selves first, we cannot open our mind's eye. This is how the roshi's words struck me. I felt his words about disposing of my body as a spur in my side. Today, I send my own disciples off to the monastery with a ten-thousand-yen note attached, for the disposal of their corpses.

The next morning, when it was still pitch dark, I went to the roshi's room to bid him a formal farewell, and then I let myself out the back door and stepped down onto the earthen floor at the entrance way. A novice monk is not allowed to use the front door. When I reached for my straw sandals, I heard Roshi come out behind me. Because Roshi was always one to stand on his dignity, and not the type to see novice monks off at the door, it surprised me to see him come out through the kitchen. What's more, he stepped down onto the dirt floor, squatted at my feet, and made to tie the strings on my straw sandals.

Embarrassed, I drew my foot back and protested, "No, that's all right. I'll do it myself."

"Here, give me your foot," he urged, pulling my leg toward him. After he had tied the strings on my sandals, he tapped his fingers on the knots and said, "Do not thoughtlessly untie these strings."

Of course, once I reached the monastery and received permission to enter, I would untie the strings on these straw sandals. What he was saying, I understood, was not to ever lightly loosen the strings of the vow to practice. Again, I trembled under the strength of my own resolution as I sank into a deep bow before Roshi and then set out on foot through the still dark morning for the meditation hall at Daitokuji, in Kyoto.

the meaning of courage

WHEN A MONK aspiring to enter a training monastery reaches the entrance hall, he takes off his wicker hat and places it out of the way in a corner, climbs up the step, and announces himself. In a large Zen temple, there is a vast entrance hall and a step that gives in to a wide stretch of corridor beyond. Although there may be dozens of monks in training within the heart of the temple, not a sound is heard in the tomblike stillness. The monk calls out in a long, loud voice, "I beg your favor," in a form established many long years past.

The aspirant monk feels his own voice sucked up into the depths of the monastery. Presently an answer rises from the distance, "Who is it?" A monk appears, wearing a cotton robe and looking very experienced. "Where have you come from?" he demands to know.

The young novice places his hands politely before him on the step, along with papers that he has brought with him. Included in the papers are a record of his own personal history, a letter requesting entry into the monastery, and a statement in which he pledges to sacrifice his life for practice, all written with brush and ink and enclosed in an envelope.

With great formality, the newcomer states his name and identifies the prefecture, town, and temple from which he comes and priest under whom he apprenticed. He promises that he has come to this place because he would like to assume the mantle of training and hang his bowl, staff, and robe on a hook in this training hall. He then asks that his request be made known.

The applicant is bid to wait as the monk disappears into the back. Returning after some time, the monk categorically does *not* say, "You are most welcome here. Please step inside." Instead, without fail, he conveys the verdict that the newcomer's request is refused. He might say, for example, that the training hall is full at the moment or that, because provisions in the monastery are extremely meager at this time, another monk could not possibly be accommodated.

In my own case, while my present weight is 150 pounds, back then I weighed less than 90 pounds and appeared to be nothing but skin and bones when I first begged entrance into the monastery. I was turned down with this excuse: "Your health appears to be extremely delicate. You would not be able to keep up with the intense training at this monastery. Please apply at another training hall."

There are some forty professional training halls throughout the country, but a monk will be rebuffed wherever he goes. Upon rejection, he takes the envelope, which has been thrust back at him, and retires into a corner, out of the way of passersby. He takes up his post on the step, doubled over, forehead down to the ground in earnest supplication until he is granted permission to enter the monastery.

Bodhidharma, an Indian monk who lived in the sixth century C.E., founder of the Zen school, was the twenty-eighth ancestral teacher in line from Shakyamuni Buddha. It is said that when Hui-ko (known in Japanese as Eka), who was eventually to become the successor to Bodhidharma and the second great Chinese ancestor, came to seek the teaching, Bodhidharma utterly ignored him. Hui-ko stood at the gate and refused to move until Bodhidharma turned his way. Day after day, Hui-ko stood his ground. Snow began to fall on the ninth day of December, and it piled up around his knees, but still he did not budge. Finally, Bodhidharma turned to look at Hui-ko and demanded, "What are you doing here?"

Upon hearing the long awaited voice of the master, Hui-ko, shedding tears of gratitude, declared his intention to practice. Bodhidharma responded with the words, "The incomparable, marvelous way of the buddhas can be attained only by eternally striving, practicing what cannot be practiced, and bearing the unbearable. How can you, with your meager virtue, little wisdom, and with your shallow and arrogant mind, dare aspire to attain the true teaching?"

Thus, Hui-ko was told that with his little insight and few resources and with his inconstant and conceited mind, he was not capable of carrying out the kind of practice necessary to awaken to truth and real peace of mind. In answer to Bodhidharma's allegations and in proof that his intention to practice was in no way frivolous, the story goes that Hui-ko drew forth a woodman's hatchet from its sheath at his hip and cut off his left arm at the elbow. It was only when he placed the severed arm before Bodhidharma that he was at long last granted permission to practice under the master.

Rooted in this tradition, the rites of passage into practice are, even today, some fifteen hundred years later, extremely rigorous. I knew from the beginning that I, too, would have to comply with the rules of the tradition. Thus I first crawled through the gate resigned to undergo the unavoidable ritual.

Yet, even as rituals go, this one was a bit rough. Soon after my initial rejection, another monk emerged, wielding an oak stick. "Despite the fact that you were just denied entry into this temple, you persist in making a nuisance of yourself by displaying your unsightly form before our entranceway," he said. "I ask that you immediately leave the premises."

Up to this point, the language had been polite enough, but even with this new verbal onslaught, I did not withdraw. I maintained my position, not moving a muscle.

"Hey, you! What's the matter—are you deaf?"

The monk followed up his tongue-lashing with jabs, kicks, thrusts, and all manner of blasphemy, and I soon found myself hurled bodily out the gate. When I peeked up and saw that the monk had disappeared inside and the coast was clear, I skulked back, like a cat out to filch, and resumed my cowering pose on the step. This whole scene was enacted repeatedly.

My patience held out in the beginning because I knew this ritual was one that I had to weather somehow, but gradually, as it went on and on, I began to get irritated: "Weren't they being unnecessarily rough considering they were dealing with someone who was not putting up the slightest resistance?" By evening, however, these sentiments, too, had vanished, and I was left feeling wretched and pitiful. Then I grew plaintively sorry for myself: "Why am I letting them treat me like a worn-out rag? Why must

I hold this miserable posture in front of this blasted doorway? Maybe both of my parents are dead, but I could still go back to Toyama. I have a few relatives left there. I can live without this cruel treatment."

All of this and much more ran through my mind.

When I was ordained, I had felt some measure of determination to carry on with a strong practice. Later, when Roshi told me, "This is nirvana money. It is for the disposal of your remains," I had made a resolution that sent a chill through my body. Then, when Roshi tied the strings on my straw sandals and urged, "Do not untie these strings thoughtlessly," hadn't I laid resolve upon resolve, hadn't I again made up my mind to do it? And now here I was, less than a day later, my mind vacillating, wondering why I had to be in this place, in this pitiful state.

I think that the human will is very weak indeed. Without having disciplined oneself, one cannot trust one's own willpower. It is very easy to waver. When I saw my own wavering, I understood for the first time the significance of being made to keep crawling back into that entrance hall. This repeated crawling back is called "being kept standing in the garden." Kept standing in the garden, the monk is forced to renew his original resolution, to strengthen that resolution, to resolve again, and to bolster that resolution still further. It is for this reason that he is kept at bay before the entrance hall.

All my teeth—not so strong to begin with!—felt loose, and the blood surged to my face. I thought my eyes were going to pop out of my skull, and my lower back, which had been bent so long in prostration, would break loose at the sockets. It was still cold when I arrived at the meditation hall on the first of March, as winter was particularly bitter in Kyoto that year. The chill commenced at my toes, pierced my feet, which were wrapped in wet sandals, and stole its way above my knees so that all feeling in my legs was lost.

To take the unsettled self in hand, under whatever conditions, and return to the mind with which one set out; to pick oneself up again, after the mind changes, weakens, and breaks down, and stiffen the determination; to carry through the oft-reconstructed original vow—isn't this the meaning of courage?

what am i doing here?

WAITING OUTSIDE that entrance, I was forced to revise my definition of courage. When I was young, I would try to demonstrate my bravery by attacking others, but this is not courage. Such aggression is, rather, like that of a puny dog with a loud bark. True bravery is pulling together one's weak mind and holding to one's original purpose. In order to maintain that hold, one must question oneself, "What am I doing here?"

While I was kept standing in the garden, a variety of thoughts drifted through my mind. I reflected that each person who finds his way into this training hall to practice is born different from the others. Each one comes into the world with different abilities, has different experiences and education, thinks different thoughts; no two are alike. If every one of the multifarious individuals who enter the training hall were to assert their own way, to insist that "This is what *I* think, how *I* do it," how on earth could practice go on?

As the saying goes, "Pour new wine into new wineskins." If it is with an eye toward self-transformation through practice that one pours one's body into the training hall, the new vessel, then it is necessary to first throw down all of one's past experiences, knowledge, and social status. One must become completely empty and enter the training hall with a humble and meek heart. In the corner before the entrance hall, the novice monk is forced to think all of this through and prepare to act accordingly.

On the evening of my third day to be held standing in the garden, a monk appeared to deliver a message, "It has been observed that since the day before yesterday, you have remained as you are before the entranceway, even while being subjected to verbal abuse and physical assault, and it has been determined that you do seem to harbor some measure of a desire to practice. For this reason, you are requested to step inside. However, as you have not been formally granted permission to train here, you are advised to remain on your guard." These were the words with which I finally made it through the front door.

The room I was allowed to enter was composed of a wall on one side and paper doors, left wide open, on the other three sides. I placed the box that I had carried on my back before the wall, and, facing the wall, I began to do zazen. I had no way of knowing who might be looking in at me from the other three directions. I could not afford to be careless.

I was served three meals a day and given bedding each night, but I was kept in this room for five more days; thus I was subjected to a total of eight days of intense self-interrogation. I asked myself over and over, "What am I doing here? What is it I am going to do?" Under the force of my own questioning, I was compelled to revert always to the starting point, to the heart with which I had set out.

Again and again I returned to the take-off point; over and over I reiterated my original resolve. I believe that courage is upholding what you have once decided to do and enduring all troubles encountered along the way. To sustain and carry out that original intention—just this, in itself—is real courage.

living out belief
in infinite power

THUS DID I ENTER Daitokuji Monastery, where I was to remain for the next fifteen years. During that period, I did zazen practice, and I eventually received the seal of Dharma transmission from my master—and I made countless blunders. It was due not to reasoning but to actual personal experience that I was able to persevere with this kind of practice even through all my failures. It was having to live out my belief that made me break through with desperate concentrated effort, without grumbling. Rather than collapse when I found myself up against a wall, however formidable, I reexamined and reassessed, and then pushed on. I think the courage to persist in this way was the result of those very first lessons I was taught when trying to gain admittance to the monastery.

Hakuin Zenji, who is considered the highest peak in the world of Rinzai Zen Buddhism, asserted that three essential elements are necessary to the realization of practice, or, indeed, to any endeavor: the great roots of belief, great doubt, and great determination.

"Belief" is belief in your own teacher and in the truth for

which he or she stands. It is, in the final analysis, belief in the limitless power of buddha-nature, which is by nature within you yourself.

While the next ingredient, doubt, may appear to be the exact opposite of belief, it actually signifies the constant awareness of your own unripeness and the consciousness of a problem that you hold always within yourself. The innate force of humankind, buddha-nature, has given birth to a marvelous tradition of wisdom, and you believe firmly in this wisdom. But reflecting upon your own immaturity and being unable to accept it creates a contradiction that stays with you constantly, as a problem.

You then must proceed with great determination, which means sticking to practice with true courage. In the Japanese language, *determination* is composed of two ideographs that carry the respective meanings "to be angry" and "aspiration." Your anger is not directed toward someone else. Indignant with yourself over your own weakness and immaturity, you employ the strong whip of aspiration; this is determination.

It was not through books and sermons that I learned about Hakuin Zenji's three requirements for the fulfillment of any goal. I was, instead, made to actualize these essentials in my day-to-day life. For this I am very grateful. I had only halfheartedly existed for the first twenty years of my life, and had I not been forced to live out these essential components—belief, doubt, and determination—I could never have persevered through anything like Zen training.

To believe in your teacher, in your seniors, in the tradition is, in other words, to believe in yourself. You must puzzle out your own unripeness. What's more, you must continue, standing firm through any trials that crop up.

Regardless of the time, regardless of the place, without these three components you cannot carry anything through to completion. I firmly believe that no matter what changes occur in the world, these are the three pillars that will support anything we hope to accomplish.

Schoolteachers often see it as their sole duty to entice children to take an interest in studying. Many parents believe the ability to parent lies in rearing children who cry out as seldom as possible, who chafe as little as possible.

I ask you all to consider this carefully, though. Is our society, into which these children will eventually enter, an understanding society? It is a world in which each individual's mind is completely full of their own affairs; it is not a world in which everyone tries to empathize and treat others with care and concern. Quite the opposite, it is a society replete with people who relish the failures of others, who savor the poverty of the next-door neighbor as they savor a tender morsel of duck meat. Regrettably, our actual society is by no means our ideal society. When children are brought up by teachers who seek always to entertain, to sympathize, and to allow their students to have their own way, and by parents who try in any way they can to prevent their children from knowing pain and inconvenience, what happens to them when they are thrown out into the kind of world we have? Isn't it the case that many sink into a more or less daily round of confusion and frustration and disappointment?

I wonder why it is that parents, teachers, and other adults do not try to provide children earlier with the opportunity and the training to realize for themselves the power inherent within themselves, the power we all possess to stand up and work it out ourselves in times of trouble. Only when we taste frustration does the spirit of intrepidity, the resolution to rally and march on over every obstacle, arise from our innate force, from our inherent power.

And this is exactly what the training of a Zen monk provides.

part two

TRAINING

a heart that does not move

Y<small>EARS AGO</small>, I was approached in London by a man who had been doing zazen for six or seven years with this question: "I am continuing with my zazen because I want to attain the heart that does not move, but I just can't seem to attain it. Even today, when I was on my way to meet you, somebody stepped on my foot in the subway. That person didn't even bother to say 'Excuse me' or 'I'm sorry,' but just went on as if nothing had happened. I tried hard to restrain myself, to keep my heart still, but I just couldn't help getting peeved. Please show me just how to do zazen so that I can find the heart that does not move."

I answered him, "You've already got a heart that does not move! Despite the fact that quite some time has elapsed since you had your foot stepped on, from then until now, your heart has not moved a step away from the place where you got angry. If you think that a still heart is one that does not move regardless of what you encounter, and if that is what you really want, there is no need for you to cultivate it anew."

"Then what is a mind that is truly still?" asked the man in surprise.

"The truly still mind, with which you were born, is the mind that moves freely. Without ignoring anything, it reacts wholeheartedly to everything it encounters, to everything on which it reflects. And yet, for all that, it is the mind that is never seized by anything, but is always ready to react on the spot to whatever it encounters next. The mind that is still is the mind that never forfeits its freedom and is able to constantly keep rolling and rolling and rolling."

This fellow was quite convinced by my answer to his question, and, pledging to do zazen ever more diligently, he went off. I gather he still continues today in his devoted effort to awaken to the "heart that is still," the mind that moves freely.

This man's case is only one example of the way in which, intent on single-heartedly pouring ourselves into something, we are apt to get hung up. No matter how enthusiastically we throw ourselves into this instant, if we cannot flow with the tide as it shifts, we are not in single-pointed concentration, not in samadhi.

The word *samadhi* carries within itself two absolutely contrary meanings: "perfect reception" and "perfect non-reception." In order to "perfectly receive" each instant as it occurs, it is necessary to "perfectly not-receive" the previous instant and the future instant. No matter how accurately and in what detail a mirror may reflect what is before it in one instant, should it be turned to face a new direction, the previous reflection will disappear without a trace and the mirror will faithfully reflect what is newly before it. Likewise, in its power to always perfectly receive what is at hand and to perfectly not-receive what is not at hand, the heart functions doubly. For this reason, from times of old, the heart has been likened to a mirror. The state in which this power functions to receive everything perfectly, just as it is—that is to say, the heart of perfect nonreception that does not get caught up—is called "the heart that is still," or simply *Zen*.

The mind that neither ignores anything nor attaches to anything is not something that is obtained through training. It is the natural "power" with which you entered this world. Those of us who are called Zen monks enter the monastery in order to awaken through practice to this power that we inherently possess, to freely demonstrate it, and to bring it to life.

getting to know my own idiocy

I HAVE HEARD it said, in critical observation of falling in love and getting married, that "Marriage is moving from beautiful misunderstanding into tragic understanding." This phrase sums up certain stages in the process of Zen practice as well. Again I say that it would not be an exaggeration to characterize my own life up to now as simply a succession of realizations of my own misunderstanding (misunderstanding that was not even beautiful!) and a process of getting to know my own idiocy.

For a person strong in his cravings, clinging to his narrow experience and knowledge as the supreme law, caught in a ravine between feelings of superiority and inferiority, between building and destroying an ideal self-image—to uncover one's own misconceptions is a task more easily described than accomplished.

There was once a great Chinese man of Zen named Chao-chou. When Chao-chou was fifty years old, his master, Nan-ch'uan, died. After three years of mourning, Chao-chou, at age sixty, set out on a twenty-one-year-long pilgrimage that took him throughout China. At the age of eighty, the extraordinary Zen master Chao-chou settled in a temple called Kuan-yin-yuan, where he guided monks and lay persons in the Dharma until his death at one hundred and twenty years of age.

One day a monk in training came to Chao-chou's temple and inquired, "What is the most solid, most unbreakable thing in this world?"

Chao-chou replied, "If you feel like insulting me, go right ahead and insult me as you please. If your initial insults do not suffice, pour on still more abuse. If you want to spit on me, go right ahead and spit to your heart's content. If spitting isn't enough, go and dip up some muddy water and slosh that on me as well."

At first glance, the answer may not seem to fit the question. Chao-chou is saying, though, that no matter how much scorn you fling upon it, this unborn buddha-nature, which cannot be hurt or sullied, is the soundest thing of all. It may appear that the hearts of some people are easily hurt. In fact, it is merely the affectations, the impurities that have been heaped upon the heart, not the pure heart with which they are born, that are injured.

Most people create sharp distinctions between good and bad, not realizing that these distinctions are meaningless artificialities. They labor under the mistaken view that practice consists of throwing out the bad and searching for the good. In so doing, they misplace their efforts and waste their energy. Holding their ideals dear, trying to become the ideal selves they picture in their minds, they fail to see the value of what is already within them. Indeed, it is not easy to take a collection of such people and lead them to awaken to the dignity that is the very root of humanity!

For this reason, before entering the monastery, the novice lives the life of a young monk, a stage in which he must pass through many gates of self-denial. I do not mean denial of the original self. I mean, rather, facing head-on and acknowledging, no matter how bitter, the unripeness and the artificialities of the self in its existing circumstances: denial of the self in its present state and recognition of the dignity of the original self.

The sixth ancient teacher of the Zen sect, Hui-neng, who lived from 638–713 C.E., came from Hsin-chou, in the south of China, a part of the country considered barbarous in those days. Hui-neng, who had lost his father when he was very young, supported his mother by gathering firewood in the forest and selling it in the town. One day when he was making his peddling rounds, Hui-neng happened upon a house where someone was chanting the Diamond Sutra. When Hui-neng heard the chanting, his mind suddenly opened, the aspiration for enlightenment arose within him, and it came to be that he climbed Yellow Plum Mountain to call on the fifth ancient teacher, Master Hung-jen.

Hung-jen saw at a glance that this visitor, Hui-neng, was a godsend. Yet when he heard that Hui-neng had come from Hsin-chou, in the south, he deliberately insulted him, asking, "How could a beast from Ling-nan expect to practice and become a buddha?"

Hui-neng did not color or flinch, but replied boldly, "There may be a distinction in the way humans lead their lives in the north and in the south, but for essential buddha-nature, there is no distinction of north and south."

When Hung-jen heard this answer, he knew that Hui-neng would succeed him in the Dharma.

Spiritually, we Zen monks are really descendants of the beasts of Ling-nan. Although we don Buddhist robes and live inside monasteries, we do not readily manage to

getting to know my own idiocy

shake off all our ornamentation and get beyond our easily injured impurities.

Now let us talk a little bit about what kind of lifestyle young monks, as we have just described them, lead inside the monastery.

routine
in the monastery

THE USUAL DAY begins at 3:00 A.M. with the sound of a ringing handbell and a voice shouting, "Kaijo!" ("Get up!"). The monks jump out of bed and pour from a small bamboo dipper into their palms the three scoops of water that they are allotted to rinse their mouths and wash their faces. They go to the toilet, put on their robes, and present themselves in the main Buddha hall.

Each action of each person is orchestrated so that the group works together as a whole. When the gong sounds in the main hall signaling the monks to appear, the leader of the zendo, the hall where the monks actually live, rings his small bell and everyone files out in silence. The morning sutra chanting in the main hall lasts about one hour.

At four in the afternoon on the last day of the year, priests make a chanting round throughout the entire temple, beginning in the main Buddha hall and finishing in the kitchen, where Idaten is enshrined—Idaten can circle the earth in a flash, and thus is the god in charge of finding food for those in practice. Years ago, when I was just beginning to learn the sutras, I was first set to making this end-of-year round of chanting through the temple. Soon after

I had finished, Zuigan Roshi, without warning, inquired, "With what mind did you chant those sutras?"

I lost my bearings completely; I was at a loss for what to say that would please the roshi. Then, when I hastened to respond with a good Zen answer, "I chanted with no-mind," I got a sharp reprimand.

"You fool. Why don't you chant in gratitude: 'Thank you for giving me this year to practice in peace'?"

There was still another time when Roshi bellowed at me, "Your voice trembles because you are trying to be good at reading the sutras. You are simply to chant the sutras with all your might."

Sutra chanting is one activity that afforded me countless opportunities to meet my own mistaken notions head-on.

After the morning chanting, the monks return to the zendo and the zazen period begins. At the clang of a special bell, they set out for *sanzen*, a private meeting with the teacher. One by one, they go in to meet the roshi face to face. What takes place now is not a convivial meeting between equals but a question and answer session. Each monk has received from his teacher a *koan*, which he must answer at this private meeting. (A koan is a "problem," taken from the words and actions of Shakyamuni Buddha and his successors in the Dharma and meant to stimulate awakening.) The monk must master the true meaning of the koan through earnest zazen, not simply by thinking about it.

When the sanzen period is finished, it is breakfast time. For the first four years I lived in the monastery, the food we ate did not appear to be food at all; gradually the diet moved toward what we could call traditional. Even then our gruel consisted of round, unprocessed barley, not the pressure-steamed and dried barley usually used in cooking. Gruel is so much the standard morning fare in Zen monasteries that the very word for breakfast is derived from this dish.

Regardless of how long unprocessed barley is boiled, it does not thicken the water, so that the end result amounts to nothing more than salt water in which grains of barley have settled at the bottom. Along with this gruel, for about three years, we were served nothing but two smelly, brackish slices of what were called "perpetual pickles." We would carefully suck the saltiness out of those two pickles as we ate, or I should say *drank*, our three bowls of gruel.

It is often said that Zen monks eat pickles without making a sound, but the truth is that the pickles that we have to chew on are not crunchy. No matter how frugally and gingerly one licks at such a pickle to make it last, before he knows it, the pickle has dissolved and slid down the throat.

It is indeed the case, not only with eating pickles, but with every movement in the dining hall—raising and lowering the chopsticks, picking up and setting down one's bowl, sipping on hot gruel—that absolutely no sound is allowed. Whispering being out of the question, all action is orchestrated with certain designated gestures and the sound of wooden clappers. The dining hall, along with the bath and the toilet, are known as the three halls of silence, where quiet is strictly enforced. It goes without saying, of course, that silence is always maintained in the meditation hall.

All the fledgling monks reside together twenty-four hours a day, each in his assigned space of one tatami mat, in a hall with no partitions, so that there is practically no such thing as private time or private space. Consequently, the only occasion when one is completely alone is in the toilet, and so requiring the monk to maintain silence even there is probably the only way he can be prevailed upon to continue being mindful uninterruptedly.

Bath day in a monastery occurs on every date of the month with a four or a nine. The monks not only take baths on this day but wash clothes, mend their robes and kimonos, and take care of any personal affairs that have arisen. At any rate they get a bath only once every five days.

No matter who a person is, if he rises early and goes to bed late, doing zazen and manual labor day in and day out, he will find the pleasure of stepping into a bath like an ascent to heaven. His spirits rise to exhilaration despite himself. For this reason, the bath is one of the three halls of silence.

But let us return to the dining hall. It is important that quiet be the rule here because regardless of how poor one's food is, it is easy for a monk to allow his mind to wander. Indeed, I might even say that the poorer the fare, the more likely it is that the mind will wander.

After breakfast, the monks clean inside and outside the dojo before setting out, just after 7:00 A.M., on their begging rounds. Days for begging alternate with days on which the master gives a talk, so that if the talks are given on the second, the fifth, the seventh, and the tenth of the month, then the first, the third, the sixth, and the eighth will be begging days. As there are seven training halls in Kyoto, the schedule is set up so that monks from neighboring monasteries do not go out to beg on the same day.

Year-round the mendicant monks weave their way through the city streets, their bare feet wrapped in straw sandals. They are not permitted to stand at the doorways of the houses they pass, but instead they form groups of three and walk single file, some thirty meters apart, chanting *"Ho!"* in loud voices as they move.

The houses in Kyoto are narrow, deep, and close together, like a row of eels. I was taught by an elder monk that we should walk at a great enough distance apart from one another so that the lady of the house who is in the backyard hanging out clothes can hear the *"Ho!"* of the lead monk, wipe her wet hands, prepare some small change or some rice, and make it to the front door at least in time to catch the third monk in line.

We are living now in a time of plenty, a time in which it is not difficult to accept money and goods from others. Almost all of the monks who went out to beg right after our defeat in the War, however, felt in their hearts a deep reluctance to engage in this practice. I, too, found it very hard to simply hold my head down and, without reserve, accept the small change held out to me.

The red-light districts—euphemistically called the flower districts—were still in existence in those days, and one time, as we were begging in such an area, some loose coins were thrown down to us from a second-story window by a girl of the establishment and her customer. A monk who had only just graduated from the university and entered the monastery grabbed the change without thinking and made to throw it back. Upon returning to the temple, he received a sound scolding from the senior monk, who spelled out in no uncertain terms the twofold meaning of the practice of begging. On one hand, it is a practice of tolerance or patience for the monk; on the other hand, begging provides others with the opportunity to throw down their covetousness. In the practice of mendicancy, benefit for oneself and benefit for others function together as the two wheels of a cart, and the young monk was told that he had acted thoroughly without prudence.

I overheard this monk being reprimanded, and the

words touched me deeply. It occurred to me then that the *"Ho!"* we shouted while begging meant "Dharma" and that we were walking our course, spreading the Dharma throughout the world. I then proceeded to go begging with the notion that I was purifying the area as far as my *"Ho!"* would reach, just as if I were a giant vacuum cleaner. One day when I was visiting my teacher, Zuigan Roshi, I happened to express these sentiments, thereby earning for myself a thundering roar.

"Fool!" he cried. "Don't delude yourself. That *'Ho!'* you're shouting stands for the bowl you are carrying to receive the alms. Just become that bowl. Don't worry about who is doing what for what reason or about what anyone is receiving or about anything else. Just go out begging without seeking anything, like flowing water, or like a cloud blown by the wind."

It was thus that another of my silly notions met its demise. In the course of spiritual practice one is apt, from time to time, to get sidetracked down various lanes of warped and preposterous impressions.

When the monks return from begging, after 10:00 A.M., it is time for lunch. This meal consists of barley-rice, miso soup with greens, and two pickles. Approximately one part rice is added to bind nine parts unprocessed barley. After the mixture is boiled to its softest possible consistency, it is mashed with a ladle so that the crushed barley becomes at least a bit sticky. Unmashed, the barley will remain crunchy and quite inedible. For supper, the leftovers from lunch are thrown together to form a kind of hodgepodge. When the monks eat too much barley rice at lunch, extra water must be added to the hodgepodge at supper, making for an especially watery concoction.

Lunch is followed by a period of manual labor, called

samu. Tasks might include working in the monastery vegetable garden, pruning shrubs and trees, pulling weeds, and splitting firewood. Work is given special emphasis in monastic life, and the monks are constantly cautioned not to consider the weight of a job in relative terms but to simply drop all analysis and apply themselves wholeheartedly to the task at hand.

Pai-chang, who lived in ancient China from 720–814 C.E., is given credit for establishing the standard for regulations followed in Zen temples. This Master Pai-chang continued working even after he had reached the ripe old age of eighty. When his disciples, who were concerned about his health, hid their master's tools, Pai-chang was forced to quit working. At the same time, however, he also quit eating. When his disciples begged him to take sustenance, he answered them with words that are now famous: "A day without work, a day without food."

Once when I told this story to a student he remarked, "I see. Those who don't work shouldn't eat. Right?"

While the two statements, that of Pai-chang and of the student, may appear to be the same, they are, in fact, completely different. The difference between facing someone else and saying, "Those who don't work shouldn't eat," and saying of oneself, "If I don't work, I don't eat," is the difference between heaven and earth. The former is a seed of aggression and dispute, while the latter is a deep precept rising from within oneself.

After the work period and the "medicinal" supper of hodgepodge (the word for supper is literally written "medicine stone"), the monks enter the zendo and do zazen until 9:00 P.M. During this period, they have another formal private meeting with the master. At 9:00 P.M., special sutras are read before "bedtime," the literal meaning of

lowing a plain vegetarian diet helps to still the mind to some degree and is, I believe, necessary.

In the zendo lifestyle, private ownership is strictly limited. The monks carry out their lives in the barest necessities: loincloth, thin cotton undergarment, waistband, and unlined kimono.

Even in wintertime, there is no thick or lined kimono. I myself never owned an undershirt until I reached my mid-thirties. There was slightly thicker cotton wear for winter, but still only the thin undergarment, unlined kimono, and robe, so that the only place on the body where the wind did not directly strike was around the middle where the belt was tied. It was as if we were living naked, with most of the body always exposed to the air. Because one feels the cold most acutely upon being routed out of bed in the mornings, in the dead of winter, the monk hurriedly chills his body—because once the skin is thoroughly chilled, he hardly feels the cold. To do zazen in the winter, I found, is to really know the cold air, as it moves up through the sleeves to be slightly warmed by the body, then up from the chest, and out to the chin in a lukewarmish flow.

Regardless of the season, the monks wear socks only for special ceremonies. Both the straps of the wooden thongs, which are made of braided bamboo bark, and the strings of the straw sandals rub and harden the skin on the feet, so that the hide on a monk's instep is even thicker than the skin on another person's heels.

Living a life of such physical deprivation, sleepiness is like a chronic illness, and the stomach is hungry year-round. Even the person of considerable desires undergoes a simplification: his craving is limited almost entirely to the desire for food and for sleep.

Elderly ladies, especially, would bow with respect when they saw us out with bare feet in straw sandals, making our begging rounds over icy winter streets. To be frank, though, after the first year or so, most monks become accustomed to monastery life, and the physical rigors cease to be of much consequence. Indeed, the most distressing aspect of training is not the physical suffering but the spiritual agony that invariably accompanies the private dialogues with the teacher. This distress decidedly *does not* disappear after a year.

The heart of the encounter with the teacher is the student's presentation of a koan. For illustration, I will use one of the most famous koans, "Show your original face before the birth of your mother and father." This koan asks, in other words, "What was your true form before your parents gave you birth?"

Some of you will submit that the question is a ridiculous one, but the monk who is given this koan—and knows that he must, without fail, take a solution in to his teacher the following morning—is compelled to work on it as if for dear life. Going at it in desperation, the first thing he realizes is that, while the physical body is passed on from parent to child, life itself continues infinitely. No child is born after the parent's death. Fascinated by the death of the physical body, we make our divisions—the life of the parent, the life of the child, my life, your life—but in reality, even if we endlessly retrace the past, the life that we are living now is infinite continuity, and we cannot pin down any beginnings for it. We can understand this much through simple reasoning alone.

Furthermore, the great functioning of this life is the functioning of the heart. To think of it in purely logical terms, the question arises: Transcending this thing one calls "myself," what is the substance of the life that continues eternally? Going beyond the self that we distinguish on the basis of small differences—differences in facial features, in personality, in abilities—*what is the original and constant true self?* Everyone at least eventually realizes that this is the question of the koan.

Even though the practitioner knows this much, he still has quite a hard way to go before he can say to the roshi, "*This* is my real form." Almost inevitably, he starts out proffering all manner of empty theories. The teacher, in the beginning, just listens in silence and rings his bell, indicating that the meeting is over and the next person in line must make his entrance.

In due course, however, the teacher will shout, "I'm not asking for explanations! Get rid of your theories and *show me* your original face!" The monk winds up at his wits' end.

The monks are not assembled in one hall and then commanded to answer the Zen question one after the other: "All right, you're next." Rather, when it is time for the private meetings, the monk on duty brings a small bell out to a location halfway between the zendo and the roshi's interviewing room and leaves it there. The roshi, holding a thick wand called a *shippei*, waits ready in his interview room. When the bell is rung, the monks, who are doing zazen, come out of the zendo, line up before the bell, and await their turn. At the roshi's beckoning, the monks, one by one, ring the bell to announce they will enter the room.

Once inside the roshi's room, master and student, completely alone, carry on the Zen dialogue. No one else is within earshot. When the roshi decides the meeting in the private room is finished, he rings his hand bell and the monk bows and departs, brushing past the person next in line to meet the teacher.

This private meeting with the teacher takes place two times each day, morning and evening, on regular days, and three times a day during the week of intensive zazen. Additionally, an especially intensive training period, called *Rohatsu O-sesshin*, is held once a year, from December 1 through the cock's crow on the morning of December 8. This week of practice commemorates the great enlightenment that Shakyamuni Buddha experienced upon seeing the morning star on December 8. During this week, no one may lie down to sleep, and there are four private meetings with the teacher each day.

No amount of theorizing will help the monk to pass his koan. And when all his reasoning is exhausted, and the bell is rung to call the monks to meet the roshi, he finds that he cannot leave his zazen mat. On regular days, the monk may be permitted to forego the meeting and whole-heartedly continue zazen. During the week of intensive practice, however, two or three senior monks with faces like the devil will come to jerk the unwilling monk off his cushion and force him to go to the teacher. The monk cannot avoid the meeting just because he has no answer to his koan.

If one looks at the pillars between the zendo and the interview room, one finds numerous scratches. These are the marks of desperation left by those monks who, lacking an answer to their koan, tried to cling to the posts when they were being dragged by their seniors to the private interview. Many times the monk who tenaciously refused to be torn from the post had his hands slapped with the keisaku. Feeling the sting of pain, he would involuntarily let go and be pulled away to meet the roshi.

The monk who finds himself before the roshi, silent, without an answer, can expect the roshi to bellow, "What are you doing here if you've got nothing to say!" and to strike him with the thick stick. Clobbered from all sides, the monk knows that even if he makes it through this one, there will be another mandatory meeting to face some hours later, in the evening, or first thing in the morning. No matter how lazy or how cunning a monk may be, he is driven into a corner so that he cannot contrive to wiggle his way through with halfhearted or makeshift means. (This style of training is found particularly in monasteries of the Rinzai sect as opposed to Soto Zen monasteries.)

As a result of such practice, I often dreamed of having satori when I was in the training hall. Upon awakening I would find, for the most part, that the dreamt experience was trifling and to no advantage. There were times, however, when the sudden realization I had in a dream held up even when I awoke. Two or three times when this happened I went in high spirits to meet my teacher, and I passed my koan.

Every night, when I finally got the opportunity to roll myself up in the oak leaf futon, rather than falling asleep, I would fall into a sort of unconsciousness, and within an instant I would be roused to start another day. Yet each time I fell into this swoon of a sleep, the very last thing to stay awake was the koan. The body sleeps, but the confrontation with the teacher first thing the next morning looms large, the sense of inquiry persisting to the end, and *"Original Face.... Original Face...."* takes over even in dreams.

Then, every morning the monk comes running through the zendo, clanging a bell and announcing, "Get up! Get up!" When one awakens to that sound, even before one is fully conscious, the sense of inquiry, *"Original Face,"* is in action. Awareness of a problem awakens first, and consciousness comes around at length. Incredible though it may seem, this was my experience training in Daitokuji.

no end to practice

E VEN FOR THOSE who follow a monastic lifestyle, it is never easy to extricate ourselves from the acquired customs that we have hauled along with us for as long as we can remember. We go along relying on self-chosen value judgments, discriminating on the basis of forms we see with our eyes, distinguishing by the sounds we hear with our ears, differentiating according to the smells we pick up with our noses. We discern tastes with our tongues, form fancies by what we feel on our skin, hold prejudiced notions in our consciousness. We compare and contrast everything we encounter. It was not a simple thing for me to emerge from this habitual kind of functioning of the mind and to purely and directly experience self and other as one.

In order to instantly apprehend situations, a phenomenon for which the philosophical term is "pure experience," I had to pass through the fear of death. I must confess that until I first experienced this in the monastery, life was nothing but continuous physical and spiritual anguish.

Let me relate something very idiotic that occurred on begging rounds one day during the period when, asleep or awake, my koan was never out of my head and my only thought was "I want enlightenment... I want enlightenment...." Unaware of what was ahead of me or behind me, I banged into something; I had run right into a cow's behind! At just the instant that I realized I had hit the cow's rump, aside from mighty astonishment, the first thing that crossed my mind was, "Oh! *This* is enlightenment!"

The most stubborn of spectators is always right within oneself, always assessing and judging one's own condition. Even when one has reached the extreme of utter exhaustion, the guardian that discriminates and cannot forget this thing called "self" gets busy whispering all sorts of petty information. In my own case, governed by the tiny knowledge and experience that I had accumulated, the guardian voice would whisper this most unwarranted warning: "If you go on like this, you might die. You'd better stop here."

Doing zazen and still more zazen, I chalked up nothing but distress and fatigue; both my head and my body began to lose their normal functioning. The thought that I would surely meet my death if I continued in this vein arose many times to interrupt my practice. But to give the conclusion before the explanation, I can tell you that matters most definitely did not take the turn that I feared. The extremes of fatigue and anguish did not give way to death, but evolved, quite contrary to expectations, into a curve that led right back to where I had started out. One night I sat, in the middle of the night, a lump of fatigue sitting on a zazen cushion, both head and consciousness were in a haze, and I could not have roused the desire for satori if I had wanted to when, suddenly, the fog cleared and a world of lucidity opened itself. Clearly seeing, clearly hearing, it was yet a world in which there was no "me"!

I cannot fully explain that time. To venture an explanation would be to err somewhere. The one thing I am sure of is that in this instant, the functioning of the heart with which I was born came into play in its purest form. I could not keep still in my uncontainable joy. Without waiting for the morning wake-up bell, I made an unprecedented call on the roshi and received permission to leave the temple for about two hours to deliver the news of my experience to Zuigan Roshi.

It did not take me an hour to walk through the black darkness to Daishuin. When I arrived, Roshi was still in bed. I crawled right up to his pillow and said very simply, "I finally saw."

Roshi sprang from his bed, examined me for a time, as if with a glare, and said, "It's from now on. From now on. Sit strongly."

This is all he said to me. From then on for the next sixteen years, until my fortieth year and Zuigan Roshi's death at age eighty-seven, whether in the monastery or back in the temple, I continued koan practice. No, really I must say that I continue still. It is not just a matter of the Zen koan, but the living koan of human life that continues without limit.

Awakening to your own original face—"enlightenment"—does not mean being able to explain yourself or knowing the source of yourself. Enlightenment is liberation from the dross of learning and experience that, without one's being aware of it, has accumulated and settled like so much sediment, or like cholesterol into one's arteries. It is the vivid, lively manifestation of the heart with which one is born—the heart that is no-form, no-mind, nonabiding, attached neither to form nor to thought, but in dynamic motion. Consequently, enlightenment is not an end point, but rather a starting point.

I have gone on at great length about life in a Zen monastery, a subject that may seem totally unrelated to your own lives. Yet all people, regardless of how their lives are structured, hold themselves dear. Everyone wants to be happy. And enlightenment is the starting point of happiness. We can use the words "true self-confidence" in place of "enlightenment." Confidence in the true self is a necessary requisite to happiness.

The power in which you can come to believe in yourself is not gained through training. It is the great power that transcends the self, that gives life to the self. The purpose of Zen practice is to awaken to the original power of which you have lost sight, not to gain some sort of new power. When you have sought and sought and finally exhausted all seeking, you become aware of that with which you have been, from the beginning—before ever beginning to search—abundantly blessed. After you have ceaselessly knocked and knocked, you realize that the door was standing wide open even before you ever started pounding away. That is what practice is all about.

Not only in places especially set up for training, but anytime and anywhere, the person who exerts himself or herself with dignity, without worrying about results and without giving in to disappointment, is a true practitioner, a true person of the Way. I believe that just this is the form of true human well-being.

part three
MASTER

what's it all about?

HAVING RECOUNTED to you much of my experience early on in training, let me now share with you some of my more recent experiences, when the roles are reversed and I have become the master. In sharing these stories, what is important to me is not that Buddhism flourish or that the Zen sect spread over the globe, but rather that each and every human being live this life completely, in the most real sense, up until the day he or she dies, with satisfaction and with peace of mind. It is with this hope that I teach.

A young relative of mine, still in his twenties, came to see me one day with a question. In his job at a trading company, he frequently has occasion to receive buyers from other countries, and in the course of friendly conversation, the visitors often ask questions about his religion. He says that when he tells them that he himself has no religion, his guests seem to react with skepticism.

"It looks as if foreigners place a lot of importance on religion," he generalized, "whereas we Japanese are ignorant of it. The truth is that young people like me only encounter religion at funerals and memorial services, and outside those times, I don't feel I have much use for it. Even feeling as I do, Roshi, is religion still important?"

What he was asking, in essence, was this: Just what is religion all about?

In Japanese, the ideographs for the word *religion* carry the meanings "main," (or "original") and "teaching." "So," I told him, "religion is at the origin of what we call life. We might say that there are various teachings and that religion is the main or most fundamental of these teachings."

When the young man heard this explanation, he said, "That means that religion is the most fundamental way of thinking about human life, doesn't it? In other words, we can interpret it to mean 'view of life,' can't we?"

I told him that we might say that, but I also asked him to tell me his view of life.

"Well, of course I think that the purpose of human life is to build something through my own efforts," he answered.

Now, this is one point of view. I myself, at one time, looked at life this way. In my youthful days, I believed that to be a human being is to be able to gain or acquire.

There are people who can run over forty kilometers in a marathon. A person knows that by training the body he or she can gain physical strength; there is an age at which this physical development is possible. By studying, you can learn anything you please. You can accumulate experiences. If you make sufficient effort, you can make friends, acquire lovers. You can get married, buy property, build a house. There is a time in your life when the world seems to be there for the taking, a time in which the view that the purpose of life is "to build something through your own efforts" may be appropriate.

Then later, as you age, you may need glasses for farsightedness, your ears start to ring, and your teeth may even fall out. When a preschooler loses a tooth, a still more wonderful tooth takes its place, but when a grown-up loses one, it stays lost! Death comes to take away the friends you have so deeply cherished. The children, for whom you have sacrificed your own food and clothing, leave the parental nest. Then retirement age rolls around, and the job over which you have taken such pains must be relinquished. You begin to forget what you thought you had learned. You lose the muscles you had laboriously built up, and they never really return. No matter how a person looks at it, he or she comes to feel acutely that human life is not a matter of gaining, but of losing.

"When that time comes, will your view of life still serve you well?" I asked my young relative.

He looked slightly sheepish as he lowered his head and allowed that he might have been a tad cocky, that perhaps it might be a good thing to at least look into what religion is all about. He even asked for my guidance.

We all conjure up notions for ourselves commensurate with our ages and circumstances in life. Out of those notions come various and sundry lifestyles. Religion, however, is not a view of life that wears well just for a certain period of time. It is a teaching that will always be valid, holding true regardless of our age and circumstances.

Everything that appears in this world constantly changes; it undergoes a period of maturing, a period of maintenance, and a return to emptiness—birth, aging, sickness, and death. Through no effort can you skirt the process of growing old. There is no endeavor whatsoever that will get you beyond death. Whatever is accumulated will be lost, whatever is born will die, whatever is built will be destroyed. A view of the essence of life is a view that helps us through our suffering as we must face it.

I believe from the bottom of my heart that what we call religion is the very most important matter for human beings. I cannot stress enough that the ultimate goal of religion, whether we call it satori or peace of mind, is for each individual to live in peace and tranquility, to live a full and satisfying life.

Every year I travel to Hokkaido to give talks, and it was after one lecture at a UNESCO assembly in Sapporo that the chairperson came to me with these remarks: "You have honored us with a lengthy and very instructive lecture, but I am an old man, and I cannot recall a long speech. Moreover, I am already a Buddhist; every morning when I leave for the office and every evening when I return home, I light incense before the altar and chant a sutra.

"The problem, though, is that I have been forced to liquidate, one by one, a number of large companies that I managed, and this disturbs me greatly. So, Roshi," he said bluntly, "I don't want to hear a long talk. I want you to tell me in a word how I can settle my disturbed mind."

Elderly people can be quite caustic sometimes, can't they? I had thoroughly lectured on the subject, and now he wants it in a word!

I responded by first asking for whom it is that he lights the incense and chants the sutras before the altar.

"Well, naturally, it is thanks to my ancestors that I am here now," he replied. "So I light a stick of incense to show gratitude to my ancestors and to Buddha."

"In that case," I told him, "from tonight on, offer two sticks of incense. One is to show gratitude to your ancestors, as you have been doing. Offer the other stick of incense to your own corpse."

We take our own "being alive" for granted, and thus get

lost in matters of circumstance, thereby effectively blinding our own good judgment. When we look at someone else's death, on the other hand, we may be quick to reflect on the transience of worldly matters.

If we turn to our own dead bodies with these same sentiments each day, perhaps we will not be so inclined to let ourselves get snagged along the way by the branches and leaves. We can free ourselves to take decisive steps with regard to more basic problems, the roots. This is what I meant when I told the gentleman to light a stick of incense to his own corpse morning and night.

When I end a lecture, I often ask everyone to please forget everything I have just said. This is because we tend to collect talk as mere data, carry it home with us, and use scraps of it as fuel for criticism of our surroundings. That which becomes the seed of criticism is not wisdom; it is nothing more than the seed of grumbling and dissatisfaction. It is so often the case that the more we feel we know about something, the more dissatisfied and plaintive we can feel.

Information collected on the subject of religion is worthless. Religion is, to the very end, something you must verify for yourself through actual practice.

Many people are willing to learn techniques that help them live their lives. But the person who seeks to confirm their life at its roots by reaching beyond technique to the fundamentals—to true religion—is exceedingly rare. I find this state of affairs most regrettable. That is why I can't help but urge you to refrain from evaluating your daily life on the basis of what you think you know, on the basis of collected data. I want you to awaken to Buddha in everything and to seek the true way of living. But make no mistake: Whether you remain in the category of a dissatisfied person or become an awakened buddha is solely up to you, dependent solely upon your own actual doing.

god is right here

IN THE SUMMERS, I often travel to England to give talks at the annual summer school sponsored by the Buddhist Society. After the talks, young mothers holding babies in their arms sometimes approach me with questions. Invariably they ask me how to go about instructing their children in the ways of Buddhism. (Unfortunately, in all my years of counseling countless people here in Japan, I have never once been asked this question.)

These women, members of societies characterized by individualism, know deep in their flesh and bones that true freedom means not relying on others. People often regard freedom as being able to have one's own way, but those from countries that have a tradition of liberalism are acutely aware that the essence of freedom is in not getting help from others. Because they understand freedom in this sense, they take one week of their enjoyable vacation time and plunge into a new way of life, disciplining themselves through often-painful zazen and listening to Dharma talks with great sincerity. At the same time, they pray that the deeply felt blessings of the Buddhism they themselves practice will also touch their children, help-ing them to lead noble lives.

One of these mothers came to me once with a story about her five-year-old daughter. As she and her husband were drinking tea on the veranda of their home one morn-ing, their daughter played in the garden with a friend. It seems that the friend turned to the daughter and said, "My grandfather just died. He's with God now, up in Heaven."

As the parents listened without really paying much attention, they heard their five-year-old daughter disagree with her friend. "No, no," she said confidently. "If your grandfather died and went to God, he's not in Heaven. God is right here inside me and you, and here in this flower, too. So your grandfather didn't go up anywhere," the little girl persisted. "My mother knows about this. She does zazen."

I told the young mother that this was a wonderful story.

When a parent cautions a child not to be wasteful, the child may respond by calling the parents stingy and point-ing out that more of anything can always be bought. Rare is the parent who has laid the ground to be able to persist in correcting their child. While growing up, inevitably, there will be times when a child abandons himself or her-self to despair. Encouraged by parents to treat themselves more gently, children often counter, "That's my business! You're not me; you don't understand me. Leave me alone! I didn't ask to be born." The parent who is rebuffed by their son or daughter in this way can say nothing.

"Compare the situation of that parent with your own situation," I told the mother in England. "Your child knows that God is within herself and within all things. Thanks to that knowledge, when your daughter is wasteful of some-thing, you can ask her if she isn't being a bit hard on the

God within that thing. With this reminder, the child can begin to see the error of her actions for herself.

"When she gets discouraged, you can ask her if treating herself unkindly doesn't sadden Buddha within, and then let her go to her room and think it out for herself. Simply reminded of what she already knows, can't the child pick herself up? It should be very easy to educate your child in this way."

This couple gets the chance to ask such questions and to receive guidance from me only once a year, for one week, but they discuss their experiences, between themselves, again and again, 365 days a year. Because it is part of their daily conversation, their five-year-old child can declare with assurance that God is inside me, and inside you, too; God is inside flowers and rocks and everything.

Words like these penetrate my mind as naturally as water penetrates the sandy soil.

is death something we cannot know?

W HILE RELIGION is certainly concerned with things other than death, let us, for the sake of this discussion, concede a hundred steps and suppose that this is not the case, that death does, in fact, have a monopoly over religion. Is there any way we can possibly think about life without considering death? Our society is very youth-oriented, and as we age, we often tend to view life as being somewhat like a tumble down a steep hill, a lonely dispatch of human life.

But this is not the only problem. Is it possible to really live our lives fully without ever looking hard at death? I do not believe it is possible. Without staring death in the eye, as the perpetual reverse side of life, we cannot live life fully and completely. I am quite convinced of this.

Regarding death as separate and apart from life, we dislike death. Thinking about how they will lose all they have accumulated, those who have made really grand efforts in life will regard death with special animosity and may not even want to consider the subject. Moreover, the general consensus among those who have thought about death is that it is something they simply do not understand. The contention is that death cannot be known because one cannot experience it while alive, and no one in this world has died and come back to talk about it. While there are people who have returned from moments of clinical death, not a soul has ever actually died and returned, some years later, to tell us about the afterworld. Some people say, then, that to think about death is a waste of time.

Steeped in this attitude, we are bound to oversimplify Confucius's meaning when he says, "We don't know yet about life, so how can we know about death?" We assume that it is possible to concentrate on living life to its fullest without looking hard at death. Thus we tend to fix a low price on the matter of death so that we can simply ignore it.

But is death really something we cannot know?

The one thing all of us are certain to encounter within our daily lives is, in fact, death. People are dying everywhere. What is more, there are the deaths of your dog, your cat, your pet canary. And what about the potted plant you bought at the nursery, wilting into demise? Or the fresh flowers you bought at the florist, withering away inside the arrangement? Then there is that special cup that you use every day and pat and treat with care: one day it slips from your hand and crashes to pieces. And there is always the "death" that is separation.

With death so prominent a part of our daily existence, how can we ignore it? Why is it that we insist on the impossibility of knowing death when death is such a routine part of our lives? How is it that we are able to so casually dismiss the subject?

The root cause for our dismissal of death is, to use Buddhist terminology, the dualistic view of self and other—"That is someone else; this is I." We tend to be indifferent to anything that we can pass off as not directly affecting our lives in the present—"What has that got to do with me?"

Although death is all around us, we regard it as something or somebody else's death. But just how justifiable is this viewpoint?

Does the sharp distinction that we make between self and other accurately characterize our situation? Is there nothing that runs between, that connects us all?

we are like water

WHENEVER I go abroad to lecture, I always go with an interpreter. On one occasion, before a talk in England, the interpreter had this to say: "Roshi, you often use the word *we* even when you are talking about yourself. But here in this individualistic English society, if I were to translate that *we* as it stands, you would lose some of your appeal. Therefore, even if you say *we,* when I am sure you really mean *I,* I would like to translate it as *I.* I hope you will give me your permission to do so."

I was amazed when I heard this. Upon reflection, I could recognize that the Japanese, as a group, do use the fuzzy term *we* when speaking, arbitrarily clumping ourselves together without the prior consent of those with whom we are identifying. And in so doing, we thereby dodge individual responsibility. Delving more deeply into the problem, however, I could not say that I really feel it is a mistake to use the word *we.*

You may assume that many entities called *I* come together to form a group called *we.* But this may not be the nature of reality.

Consider this: Suppose that a person is in a very sincere

and tranquil mood, with no anxieties, in a clear, healthy psychological frame of mind. (When one's mind is distorted and hung up, that is another story!) Suppose that person is a housewife in the kitchen in the evening, and she hears the familiar sound of her husband's footsteps as he comes home. Wiping her hands on her apron, she goes to the door to greet him. In this instant this person is— with the face of a wife, the voice of a wife, the body and movements of a wife—a wife greeting her husband.

Then, just as she reaches to take his coat, a voice from behind calls, "Mama!" She turns around and responds, "What is it?" And just in that instant this person no longer has the face of a wife, but of a mother. She looks back with the face of a mother, the voice of a mother, the gestures of a mother. Then, if a friend from the neighborhood comes to call, she receives her guest not with the face of a wife or of a mother, but with the face of a next-door neighbor.

Perhaps as you read this, you imagine me in one form, as a monk. But tomorrow morning I will visit the grave of my parents. Standing before that grave, I am nothing more than a child. One appears before one's parents as a child, before one's child as a parent, before one's husband as a wife, before one's wife as a husband. At work, the face and form one takes on depend upon the position they occupy. This is our true form.

There is no clump called "I" moving from this spot to that spot, instant by instant. Rather, through particular encounters with particular people, within each encounter, within each transition, something called "I" makes its appearance. Thus it is that what seems to be an object outside yourself is, in reality, your complement, that which gives this instant of your life its glow.

If you understand phenomena in this way, you understand why the Zen school sets up its practice so that you can attain enlightenment by looking intently into your own heart. If that heart were really yours alone, no matter how intently you continued to gaze at it, you could never awaken to universal truth. But the heart is not an individual possession; it is not yours alone.

The heart, the life that is within you, is born in companionship with the environment. Your heart is the life of the great universe. Our own hearts are the womb from which everything originates, and just as I am a manifestation of Buddha, so are you a manifestation of Buddha. Therefore, the Zen school teaches that we should not set out to know "everything"; we should investigate that which is closest at hand, our own bodies and hearts. So it is that just by looking into your own tiny mind, you can be receptive to others—not to mention that you can realize the truth of the entire boundless universe!

We are not like blocks of ice, conducting ourselves as solid individuals as we move from place to place. We are like water flowing freely, now into a four-sided container, now into a three-sided container, realizing a new birth each and every instant. Such, I believe, is the reality of our existence, and it is this sort of human existence, this sort of existence of all things in the universe, that Buddhism expounds.

It follows, then, that we are not individual "I's" gathering to form a "we," but that within the existence of "we," something called "I" arises. This, I believe, is reality.

When we are in accordance with this original form, it is possible for us to understand the death, the pain, the sadness, the happiness of another as our own.

the death
of my grandfather

THE YEAR BEFORE I was to enter grammar school, on a hot day with the sun beating down, my grandfather took me to see a local wrestling match. My grandfather always treated me most affectionately. We left in the morning, and he probably planned to be home by around noon, but, as I was very persuasive with him, we stayed out all day and did not return home until evening. As a result of staying out in the sun too long, Grandfather had a heat stroke. Even as a child just over the age of six, I could realize that my own coaxing was the cause of my grandfather's abnormal condition.

My father, who was a doctor, did not move Grandfather to a hospital, but rather examined and nursed him at home. As this was the beginning of the Showa Period, back in the 1930s, medical treatment was quite primitive. A block of ice was placed in a tin plate, and as the ice melted, the cold water was used to cool his brow.

The whole house was turned upside down in confusion, and messengers were sent to call in relatives. It was not as simple in those days as it is now, when the family can jump into the car and drive over in response to a telephone call. After receiving the announcement, relatives had to cross the mountains on foot in their straw sandals.

I was left quite neglected as everyone gathered and, moment by moment, alternately rejoiced and lamented, according to Grandfather's condition. Seeing my relatives like this and feeling the disturbed atmosphere of the house, I was frightened. I ran away to the second floor and, lying on my belly over the stairwell, watched the scene below. As I gazed down at the hushed tumult below, I realized that Grandfather was going to die. I remember puzzling over whether or not that meant that I would not see him again.

For me, as a child, the idea that Grandfather could suddenly disappear was not an idea I could readily absorb. He had always been so present, so affectionate. While I was mulling over this matter, my mother climbed to the second floor to find me and explain that Grandfather was going to die.

"When people are dying," she said, "they get very thirsty, and so we need to give them water. Since Grandfather has pampered you more than any of his other grandchildren, you must go now and give him some water." I was half-dragged back downstairs.

I was given a wad of cotton soaked with water to wipe Grandfather's lips. I could see for myself that while his forehead was damp, his lips, which were locked tightly together, were dry and chapped, and I felt that he must be very thirsty. When I started softly wiping, drops of water settled into the seam of his lips and they became moist, but not a drop passed through and into his mouth. Figuring that I was not using enough water, I squeezed the wad of wet cotton over his mouth. The water trickled down his face, and still not so much as a drop entered his mouth.

My grandfather, who had always so enjoyed drinking his tea, and who was now so thirsty, could not open his mouth to swallow even a sip of water. The feeling that a big change had taken place penetrated deep into this child's heart and flesh and bones. Not long after, Grandfather took his last breath and we washed his body for cremation.

People once thought it would be a pity for the deceased, bound for Amida's beautiful Pure Land, to have to go carrying the dust of this world. It was with this artless feeling that the dead were given their last bath. The survivors filled a washtub with cool water to which hot water was then added.

In my house on that day, hot water was poured in the sink, a little rubbing alcohol was added, and my grandfather's whole body was wiped with a wet towel. I was allowed to wipe his chest, but the towel slid from my tiny hands, which then skidded directly across Grandfather's skin. I can still feel the sensation of touching his skin. Before, when Grandfather had let me ride on his shoulders, I could see the wrinkled skin on the nape of his neck. Under my hands, which clutched his forehead to keep from falling of, I could feel the wrinkled skin. His body was flexible and warm then, whereas now the hands that unexpectedly touched him found stiffness. The coldness of his body, a coldness completely unlike that of ice, sent a chill throughout my own body. This six-year-old child received a sharp lesson about death.

My family carried me along the narrow lanes between the rice fields as the coffin was taken away. The crematorium was not like those of today with their heavy doors like bank vaults. It was no more than a hole, through which the family shoved the coffin and through which its edge could still be seen. The hole was heaped with straw, and firewood was laid against the casket. Then the family, all together, lit pine torches and started the fire. When the straw and the firewood and the coffin started to crack and pop in the flames, we went home to await the next day, when we would gather Grandfather's ashes. Even to my six-year-old eyes, as I looked back over my shoulder at the soy-colored smoke rising from the chimney of the fire I had just helped to start, death was personal. It was not "somebody else."

Now, I was seeing my grandfather—the man I respected and wanted to emulate—being burned up. What I saw then was not someone else's death, but my own future. I am not exaggerating this incident, looking back and dramatizing it from the distance of many years. I really did, as a six-year-old child, see the future of my own body burning in that fire.

inexhaustible
dharma

S INCE I EXPERIENCED my grandfather's death, there have been two or three times that I wanted, from the bottom of my heart, to die. Perhaps you have had similar feelings. Once, in fact, I even tried to overdose on medicine, but I believe that I unconsciously kept that dose within safe bounds. I could not die. I believe that the main reason for my inner reluctance to die was my having been made to experience the death of my grandfather. My cognizance of death, as a result of that experience, was of a depth and a breadth that I could not easily leap across.

The "death" that many people know, however, is not the future death-in-earnest of their own bodies. Oftentimes, the only death they know is death as it occurs in a historical drama or a suspense film that they enjoy watching as they lie on their backs on the floor or on the sofa eating candy and snacks.

Let me relate another story, about my old grammar school teacher, a truly great man. From the second grade up through graduation, my classmates and I were fortunate to have him in charge, and he had a decisive influence on each and every one of us.

A few years ago, in commemoration of the half century that had passed since graduation, we held a class reunion. Out of some fifty classmates, more than ten had died, and the thirty-three of us who gathered amounted to almost full participation. I myself, putting aside all of my work, would not have missed it for the world. We had a banquet and spent the night at a hot spring resort, and although we drank our saké, not a soul proposed that we sing karaoke. Even as we gathered around our teacher, drinking informally together, our meeting was a serious one. Various members of the group consulted our teacher and some even asked me questions about different things affecting their lives. That it was altogether like a training seminar was due to the deep influence of our teacher.

This gentleman was a great educator, and he has continued, since his retirement, to lead an exemplary life as a member of the community. His personal lifestyle, too, is impeccable. Despite his eighty-plus years, he appeared more robust than any of his former pupils!

When the time came to retire after our banquet, all those who had gathered around to hear our teacher's words seemed reluctant to impose upon him further, so it happened that he and I were given a room to share for the night. We had placed our pillows side by side, lain down, and turned off the light when he called out, "Morinaga-san," kindly affixing the honorific *-san* to the name of the student he had taught so long ago.

"Heaven forgive me for this foolishness," he continued, "but lately I've been so afraid of dying that I almost feel it would be better not to have been born!"

The words of my teacher did not hit me lightly. On the

contrary, I recalled how diligently he had labored through-out his eighty years, and his confession touched me with all the more poignancy.

Living, as we do, a finite existence, appearing as form in this world of phenomena, we are without fail subject to the law of cause and effect, the law of karma. It is a foundation stone of Buddhist teaching that where there is birth, there is death; certain efforts bear certain results. All research of the natural sciences and of the humanities is conducted on the basis of this principle of causation. Further, in matters of everyday life, even people who don't think carefully about such things seek to live in such a way as to produce causes that bring about positive results.

There are those who have, in accordance with this law, consistently endeavored to accumulate good karma and who have met with success in their efforts. When such a person ultimately collides with the insurmountable walls of old age, sickness, and death, walls that no amount of stockpiled karma can help one to scale, they are truly disappointed.

Inevitably, the person who has taken special pride in their work meets the onslaught of old age—which renders them incapable of working as they have up to now—with special dread. The person who boasts of an exceptionally sharp intellect will be especially intimidated by a progressive dimming of the mind. The person who has lived an exemplary life as a member of society will be especially frightened to witness the siphoning away of their own physical and mental power.

Thus it is that we cannot hope to live our closing years with peace of mind simply by striving to conduct a meritorious life under this law of cause and effect.

Within Buddhism, there is a field of teaching that

applies to our finite existence within causality and that utilizes the terms *exhaustible dharma* and *created dharma*. Called the Precepts of the Seven Buddhas because it has been taught by all the buddhas who have appeared in the world, the teaching instructs us to live life attempting to plant wholesome seeds and thereby harvesting beneficial fruits. A well-known verse summarizes the doctrine:

> *To avoid doing evil,*
> *To do good,*
> *To purify the heart:*
> *This is the teaching of all buddhas.*

If one makes a deep inquiry through practice into this teaching, delving into one's own heart, which suffices to purify itself, one naturally goes beyond the category of a teaching limited to life within this body and subject to karmic retribution. It is unfortunate that people tend to interpret this kind of doctrine—sowing good seeds, reaping good fruits; sowing bad seeds, reaping bad fruits—only in its application to worldly happiness and prosperity. Of course this aim is, in itself, extremely important, but success within these limits alone does not assure the ultimate peace of mind that transcends sickness, old age, and death.

No matter what efforts you have channeled into the production of success, once your name is called, the slate of your worldly accumulations is cleared. This cycle applies not only to the human realm but to all phenomena, which must go through a time of birth, a time of abiding, a time of transition, and a time of returning to original emptiness. In the case of human beings, this is birth, aging, illness, and death. All phenomena are like bubbles, appearing and disappearing, impermanent, changing. No individual entity exists anywhere that carries on, as is, in perpetuity.

This is the Buddhist emptiness or voidness, called in Sanskrit *shunyata* and in Japanese *mu*, and the reality of this emptiness is called *inexhaustible dharma*. All being is without fail exhausted. But the voidness or emptiness, which is the very foundation of all being, is inexhaustible. That the exhaustible and the inexhaustible are not separate is expressed in the well-known line from the Heart Sutra, "Form is exactly emptiness, emptiness exactly form."

The fact is, however, that it is exceedingly difficult to see clearly for oneself that all things are in themselves empty. We can say that in order to realize the intrinsic emptiness of ourselves, we must wring from our bodies sweat of oil.

to die while alive

WHEN I BECAME a monk and entered the train-ing hall, more than anything in the world, I passionately desired enlightenment. Kyoto, where my training monastery was located, was not a land abundant with rice paddies, and so there was but ten days' supply of staple foods rationed out per month. That ten days' supply of staples included such things as corn and sweet-potato flour and, at times, an undrinkable, faded yellowish tea powder. This was our fare when I was in the training hall, single-mindedly doing zazen and seeking enlightenment.

But this experience of enlightenment did not come eas-ily. I had been educated, up until I began Zen training, to see with the eyes, hear with the ears, and think it all out with the head, and that was the only way I knew in which to proceed with my investigation. In training, however, I was informed that satori is not some sort of conclusion brought forth through my own judgments, which are dis-cerned from the outside world through the six senses (sight, hearing, smell, taste, touch, mind). Still, I could not readily grasp just how to get beyond this habitual way of perception to another way of experiencing.

Daito Kokushi, the founder of Daitokuji temple and one of the most illustrious Zen masters in Japanese history, in his final words admonished: "Be ever mindful, throughout the twenty-four hours of the day, to apply yourselves to the study of the Unthinkable." This Unthinkable is the transcending of logic or intellectual understanding, and I hadn't the faintest notion how best to throw my energy into this practice of the Unthinkable. So I just blindly went at zazen. Each night while everyone else was fast asleep, I persisted, sitting on my cushion. Unfortunately, during this period it was my duty to awaken the others in the mornings.

As I mentioned, food was very scarce, and I was already quite lean. I toiled at manual labor and practice during the day and continued zazen without sleep through the night, so that while I had every intention of remaining upright, I would wind up in a sort of fainting state, pass out and tumble off the cushion.

Monastery rising time was 3:00 A.M. every day. It must have been that I would faint at 2:00 or 2:30 A.M. Coming to with a start, I would find it past time to awaken the others. This continued for three days, until finally I was roughly reprimanded, charged with "forgetting" to wake up and thus throwing the whole monastic day out of kilter. *Densu* is the title of the position I held. I was told in no uncertain terms that in the monastic rules it is dictated that the *densu* watch the clock "just as he guards his very own eyeballs."

"Do you really have any interest in practice or not?" shouted my superior. "What do you think you're here for, anyway?"

To be asked if one really has any interest in practice is, in effect, to be kicked out of the training hall. Fortunately, however, the master took pity on me, and fellow monks kept an eye out, helping me to avoid further slips. My obstinacy did prevail, though, and I continued to practice without ever lying down to rest at night. Despite my unrelenting persistence at sitting, every night I would grow hazy and doze off so that my zazen was far from strong and clear.

Then, to make matters worse, I reasoned that taking in food would make me sleepy, so I stopped eating. As I mentioned before, meals in those days were not what could be called substantial. We took our meals formally, chanting sutras before and after. Before each meal an announcement would be made such as "Today's lunch will consist of three dumplings per person." This meant that each monk would receive three balls of pressed potato starch, each about the size of an old copper coin. There was no soy sauce or miso, and these dumplings would be boiled in salt water, of which we would each receive three bowls. To stop eating even this because it might make me drowsy was going too far.

Then, one night, all of my ammunition was exhausted.

I lost all sense of wanting enlightenment; to continue seeking satori was inconceivable. Gone was the physical and mental energy necessary to maintain a level of consciousness in which one tries to verify with the eyes and hear with the ears. The soft cushion beneath me was a steel plate. My whole body was a mass of sheer pain. It was not "I" sitting on that cushion; it was sheer fatigue. As if consciousness were lost in a fog, all was hazy.

Suddenly, under some impetus unknown to me, the fog lifted and vanished. And it is not that the pain in my own body disappeared, but rather that the body that is supposed to feel the pain disappeared. Everything was utterly clear. Even in the dimly lit darkness, things could be seen in a fine clarity. The faintest sound could be heard distinctly, but the hearing self was not there. This was, I believe, to die while alive.

At the time, there were actually no thoughts. I have no idea of the duration of this state of utter clarity, of what happened to precede or follow it. Perhaps I was roused by a sharp voice. I only know that when I came to myself, I felt tremendously happy! It was just as if I didn't know the dance of my own hands, the steps of my own feet. It never crossed my mind that this was a satori experience or that "I had kensho." Without any theorizing, I felt only the brimming joy of having had a heavy burden suddenly swept away.

Going over my experience in retrospect, in light of various passages in the sutras and in the records of the ancient teachers, I see that a verse by Shido Bunan Zenji is very fitting:

> Die while alive,
> Thoroughly die.
> Then just do as you will,
> and all is right.

The famous psychiatrist Elizabeth Kübler-Ross has collected statements from persons who have died a clinical death and then recovered to tell about it. According to these reports, when one is about to die, just in that instant, it is not only that the body, which has suffered in sickness and pain, is totally released from that suffering but that the person actually feels released from the body itself. These people reported that, although they did not know where they were, they could clearly see others gathered around their bodies, wailing or clinging to and shaking the corpse. It would appear that there may be certain slight similarities between such experiences of medical death and death in practice, but this is something I cannot confirm.

What I, and others who have gone through the experience, *can* positively affirm is that there is a state of mind that surpasses cause and effect, a state other than the one in which we seek to gain "that" by doing "this." It is a samadhi in which each instant is whole as it stands, in its totality. Each instant is reflected perfectly, as if in a mirror.

It is wonderful and necessary to throw one's energies into living in such a way as to plant, and thereby reap, the seeds of wholesome action within this limited world. Still, living a life solely based on the law of cause and effect—acting in anticipation of future or immediate results—a person will, without fail, come up against a barrier and feel despair.

By meeting what you are faced with right now, though, in this very instant, completely without judgment or evaluation, you can transcend by far all question of cause and effect. You may be working in the kitchen or sweeping in the garden or cleaning the toilet or laboring for somebody else, but you do it without consideration of its relative merit. That means simply doing with all your might, becoming one with whatever situation in which you find yourself in this instant. I would like for you to clearly know that there is this other way of living your life.

On the one hand, even though you apply yourself to and are successful in reaping benefits for yourself, without transcending the barriers of old age, sickness, and death, you will not be tranquil in the evening of your life. On the other hand, if you cling to the idea of emptiness and fall into nihilism, it is easy to make the mistake of passing your whole life in vain. But there is another way: the middle way, falling into neither extreme. This middle way is called the Dharma gate of liberation, liberation from both the exhaustible and the inexhaustible.

give yourself
to death

I WOULD LIKE TO TELL YOU one final story, a story that has moved me very deeply. It is the story of Miss Okamoto, who stayed by my teacher's side for forty years, up until his death.

Miss Okamoto, as I said earlier, quit her job in young women's education and entered the temple after the age forty as a disciple of Master Zuigan. She trained as a lay person, never shaving her head or taking the vows of a nun, but also never wearing makeup as a lay woman might. She carried out all her affairs tidily attired in baggy work pants.

It was not her intention to become a great monk, so rather than focus on the training itself, she worked hard to make life smooth for the master whom she so respected. By washing clothes, cooking, and raising fresh vegetables, Miss Okamoto ensured that he would always be available to teach the Dharma to others. Anyone who looked at Miss Okamoto would see a thoroughly self-sacrificing person.

Master Zuigan died at the age of eighty-seven, when

Miss Okamoto was sixty years old. When the final ceremony of the forty-nine-day bereavement period was concluded, she packed up her belongings and, declaring that she did not wish to be a burden to me, left the temple. She moved into the rented cottage of a different temple, where she continued to live out her years of retirement, under no one's supervision, just as she had lived when Master Zuigan was alive.

Miss Okamoto rose every morning at 4:15 and, although she had made no formal commitment to do so, cleaned the temple gardens surrounding her rented room. She cultivated vacant land and planted vegetables, which she would pickle to offer to the novice monks in training under me, to share with visitors, and to offer at the Buddha altar.

When she was already well into her seventies, feeling that she wanted to improve herself in whatever way she could, Miss Okamoto began to come inside after a day of sweeping, pulling weeds, and gardening to hear a talk and study classical Chinese literature. At other times, remembering the lectures she had heard Roshi give on various Zen works, she would open koan collections like the *Blue Cliff Record* and *The Gateless Gate*. Such was the life Miss Okamoto led.

She was a little old lady, short with a round boyish face, but her exceptionally strict, upright lifestyle had given rise to something forbidding in Miss Okamoto, and the young novice monks were never pleased when they were sent to her place on an errand.

I visited Miss Okamoto monthly, and she always seemed eager for these visits. But one day, she sent a message to the effect that she wanted me to call on her right away as she had something urgent to talk to me about.

"Here for the past half year, I've been suffering intense physical weariness," she began when I visited her. "Thinking that I had reached the age when I was growing dull, I tried to whip myself along, to keep going, but I just wasn't getting any better.

"Finally," she explained, "there seemed to be nothing to do but ask someone to take me to see a doctor. Although the doctor didn't say it in so many words, it seems that I have cancer. Since I found this out, I have been afraid of dying."

Her words were an echo of those of my old school-teacher. But not only was Miss Okamoto afraid of dying, she was also ashamed of that fear. She felt it disgraceful to fear death after having been allowed to train for so long under her teacher. She felt tremendous gratitude toward the Zen sect and toward the roshi, and it was unbearable for her to think that those around her might feel Zen practice is useless since it apparently does not even help one to overcome apprehension in the face of death.

"What in the world is the problem with the way I have practiced up until now—that death could be this frightening? Please tell me how I have been wrong in my practice," she beseeched, opening up to me as if I were her own son.

Although Miss Okamoto was twenty-four years my elder, her earnest confession prompted me, despite her years, to bluntly call to her attention something in her manner that had already been weighing on my mind.

This woman had led a flawless, commendable life, but she had always stoically gritted her teeth in an effort "to do good, to avoid doing evil." Sharply distinguishing between "good" and "bad," forever sizing up and passing judgment on the situation, she went about her endeavors to "do better," but always with her teeth clenched fast. Let me be very clear about this: The kind of effort in which one bisects good and bad, and then chooses one over the other with the intent to stack up causes for positive results does not in itself produce peace of mind.

As I explained to Miss Okamoto, you come out from your mother's womb and go into your coffin. That time in between, you call life, and perhaps you think of going into your coffin as death. But true existence is birth and death, repeating itself, instant by instant. If you look at a flame, it seems to burn continuously and give off constant light. In actuality, the wax is burning down bit by bit, and the wick that blazes in this instant exhausts itself, passing the flame farther along.

Our lives appear to be unbroken blocks of seventy or eighty continuous years, but, actually, they are just as the example we saw earlier: you are a wife when you look this way; you are the woman next door when you look that way. When you maintain the straight-forward frankness of your own mind as it comes to life each instant, even without effort, even without training, you are beautifully born with each instant. You die with each instant, and go on to be born again, instant by instant.

As I told Miss Okamoto, when you go to the kitchen to prepare dinner, be born in the kitchen. When you finish there, die. Then be born at the dining table as you eat your dinner and, when you finish eating, die there. Be born in the garden, and sweep with your broom. When you get into bed at night, die there. And when daylight comes, and you awaken in your bed, be born anew. If you have cancer, be born with cancer.

Always now—*just now*—come into being. Always now—*just now*—give yourself to death. Practicing this truth is Zen practice.

buddha life

I HAVE SEEN many people practice. But I do not know of anyone who so splendidly, so thoroughly, put my instructions into practice as did Miss Okamoto. She complied as docilely as a lamb. It wasn't even ten days before her rigid countenance had softened into a baby face, into the face of a sweet old lady. She had left behind the lifestyle in which she had to grit her teeth and try to live right.

Miss Okamoto's disease grew progressively worse, and she finally had to be hospitalized. I remember that when I called on her, the doctors and nurses all remarked that though they had worked in the hospital for many years, they had never encountered a patient like this one. By the time Miss Okamoto entered the hospital, she was greeting everybody, everything, every scene in the spirit of "one chance, one encounter."

Most people interpret this "one chance, one encounter" as applying to some very special occurrence, a once-in-a-lifetime magnificent encounter. The phrase calls to mind, for example, a tea ceremony, which happens as it happens only one time. It is generally reasoned that something that happens only once in a lifetime, a once-in-a-lifetime encounter, has to be an exceedingly special occasion, and the expression is commonly limited to this usage.

In its true sense, however, "one chance, one encounter" may occur when one encounters a stone, when one comes upon a weed, when one is cleaning the toilet or cooking rice. It refers to a state of mind in which one makes absolutely no projections of favorability or adversity, in which there is absolutely no notion of escape. To practice "one chance, one encounter" is to wholly melt within each one occurrence, and this is just the way Miss Okamoto saw her life out.

Unfortunately, I had agreed to journey to England and the United States again at that particular time, and I left feeling uneasy. I instructed my disciples to care for Miss Okamoto during my absence, but she passed away without waiting for my return. When I came back, I heard from my oldest disciple, the monk who had last attended her, about the final moments before her death. Although this was a man who seldom allowed any expression to cross his face, tears streamed from his eyes as he told the story.

Before Miss Okamoto died, she said to him, "Looking back, I have led a pretty stuffy life all these years. So I think I'll just take a ball and go out and play in the woods now." These were her last words.

We placed a pretty ball, made of colored threads, inside her grave.

I hope that you will not merely take Miss Okamoto's final words for their emotional or their literary appeal. When I heard what she had said at the last, I felt joy from the bottom of my heart. Joy, because I was confident that in her living and in her dying, Miss Okamoto had literally reached a state we can call the "samadhi of play."

If a person is working for wages, shoveling sand onto the

bed of a truck with a shovel, they may get tired. Should someone happen along and offer to help out, they will most likely be glad to hand over their shovel. But suppose a child is playing in a sand pile, scooping sand into a bucket. Should someone walk up and offer to take over for a while, that child would balk at such foolishness, "Why should I want you to take over when I'm having so much fun?"

Even the most fleeting of activities, such as the business of preparing a meal, can be the samadhi of play. When you throw your heart into preparing a fine meal, which you artistically arrange on the plates and serve up, that food is swiftly devoured and you are left with dirty dishes. To carry on in the samadhi of play does not only refer to creating a work of art that might grace a museum for a few hundred years, but to the most everyday of everyday affairs one performs. The duties of housekeeping serve as a good example. In a never-ending cycle, we clean, and the house gets dirty again. We sweep, and the dust comes back. We wash clothes, and they get soiled again.

This is not only the case with housekeeping. Look closely and you see that these are the circumstances of every activity by every human being on earth.

The samadhi of play is the state of mind in which one performs an activity without appraising its relative value, just as the child who plays in the sand would never dream of letting someone else take their place. It was with this mind that Miss Okamoto went out to the woods to play ball.

The samadhi of play is a state in which the heart transcends both the exhaustible dharmas and the inexhaustible dharmas. This is the Dharma gate of liberation, the state of mind that is liberation from both the exhaustible and the inexhaustible.

There is within you yourself eternal Buddha life. That

Buddha life appears in form, being born and dying, instant by instant, emerging in constant succession in the samadhi of play. We can clearly say that the practice of this mind state is the satori state of Zen.

Within you there is eternal life. This life arises as form and continues, instant by instant, appearing and disappearing. Moreover, this flickering, appearing and disappearing, is not the flickering of a solidified individual self; it is the sparkling appearance and disappearance of a fusion of the self and its surroundings, in union.

This is what the founder of the Soto Zen school, Dogen Zenji, meant when he said that birth and death is the life of Buddha. Birth and death is the pulse of Buddha life.

Where there are one thousand human beings, within one thousand ways of living, one thousand buddhas are revealed. Buddha is revealed through mountains, valleys, trees, and grasses, through a multitude of phenomena. The heart that can be revered in whatever form we see, in whatever direction we look, this is the true heart of Buddhism. This is Buddha life.

Personally, I understand the words *birth and death* as Great Life, dynamic and dancing lively. Throughout this book I have talked to you about this big, lively dancing life and about the process by which I have come to see my life in this way.

As I've mentioned, when I end a lecture, I often ask everyone to please forget everything I have just said. But nonetheless, it is my earnest desire that this clumsy narrative be a stimulus that may, in some way, help you to lead your own life—living each and every instant with great care, aware that *just this* is the great, dynamic, lively dancing life.

about the author

Soko Morinaga Roshi was born in 1925. After graduating from high school, he entered Zen practice. He was ordained as a monk by Zuigan Goto in 1948. From 1949 through 1963, he trained in the monastery at Daitokuji and received the seal of Dharma transmission from Sesso Ota Roshi. While actively working in the lay community, delivering talks and writing books and articles, he served as the head of Hanazono University, the primary training university of the Rinzai sect, in Kyoto. He had a long-standing connection with the Buddhist Society of London and traveled there every year to participate in the summer school jointly sponsored by various Buddhist sects. Morinaga Roshi died in 1995.

about the translator

Belenda Attaway Yamakawa is a longtime student of Zen. She lives in a temple near the Sea of Japan with her husband and two children.

also from wisdom
publications

ORDINARY MIND

EXPLORING THE COMMON GROUND OF ZEN AND PSYCHOTHERAPY
Barry Magid • Foreword by Charlotte Joko Beck
ISBN 0-86171-306-0, cloth, $22.95

Buddhist meditation and practice have proven to be beneficial
in the psychotherapeutic process, and psychotherapy is helping
many spiritual practitioners work through underlying issues of
identity, but a book that expertly examines this synthesis has
not previously been available. Dr. Barry Magid's groundbreak-
ing *Ordinary Mind* zooms in on potential opportunities and pit-
falls and brings the reader to a clearer understanding of the
path toward personal realization and fulfillment.

"An exciting and hope-inspiring work, the very reading of this
book is in itself therapeutic!"—James S. Grotstein, M.D., author
of *Who Is The Dreamer Who Dreams the Dream?*

ZEN AND THE KINGDOM OF HEAVEN

REFLECTIONS ON THE TRADITION OF MEDITATION
IN CHRISTIANITY AND ZEN BUDDHISM
Tom Chetwynd
ISBN 0-86171-187-4, $16.95

This provocative and very human work is the story of one
man's skeptical first encounters with Zen Buddhism, and how
it led him to the rich—but largely forgotten—Christian tradition
of pure contemplative prayer. Chetwynd explores the surpris-
ingly Zen-like teachings of the Desert Fathers and other Christian meditation masters whose practice stems from the very
first Christian communities—and perhaps Jesus Christ himself.

"Chetwynd's primary purpose is to unite Christian belief with
aspects of Buddhist discipline. A very thoughtful and provocative read."—*Today's Librarian*

"Engaging, illuminating, and thought-provoking."—Reverend
Priscilla Inkpen, Naropa University

DAILY WISDOM
365 BUDDHIST INSPIRATIONS
Edited by Josh Bartok
ISBN 0-86171-300-1, $16.95

"One of the basic practices of Buddhism is to remain mindful, and one way this is achieved is simply through reminders. Ranging in length from a sentence to a short page, these reminders include poetry, meditation instruction, practical advice, and thoughts on the way things are. Brilliant quotes from the likes of Ayya Khema, Alan Wallace, Milarepa, Henepola Gunaratana, Martine Batchelor, and the Dalai Lama; retain this kind of inspiration throughout the day, and peace will be yours."—Brian Bruya, Religion Editor, Amazon.com

ZEN MEDITATION IN PLAIN ENGLISH
John Daishin Buksbazen
Foreword by Peter Matthiessen
ISBN 0-86171-316-8, $12.95

"Buksbazen, a psychotherapist and Zen priest, offers practical and down-to-earth advice about the specifics of Zen meditation. The bulk of this primer is concerned with introducing the basics of *zazen*, or seated meditation: how to position the body; how and when to breathe; what to think about. Helpful diagrams illustrate the positions, and Buksbazen even provides a checklist to help beginners remember all of the steps. This is a fine introduction to Zen meditation practice, grounded in tradition yet adapted to contemporary life."—*Publishers Weekly*

A wealth of fine books about meditation, Buddhism, and your mind—
browse through them all at wisdompubs.org. While you're there, be
sure to sign up for the Wisdom Reader, our free e-newsletter,
for additional updates and offers.

WISDOM PUBLICATIONS
Publisher of Buddhist Books
199 Elm Street, Somerville MA 02144
wisdompubs.org
Orders: 800-272-4050

about wisdom

Wisdom Publications, a not-for-profit publisher, is dedicated to making available authentic Buddhist works for the benefit of all. We publish translations of the sutras and tantras, commentaries and teachings of past and contemporary Buddhist masters, and original works by the world's leading Buddhist scholars. We publish our titles with the appreciation of Buddhism as a living philosophy and with the special commitment to preserve and transmit important works from all the major Buddhist traditions.

To learn more about Wisdom, or browse our books on-line, visit our website at wisdompubs.org. You may request a copy of our mail-order catalog on-line or by writing to:

Wisdom Publications
199 Elm Street
Somerville, Massachusetts 02144 USA
Telephone: (617) 776-7416 • Fax: (617) 776-7841
Email: sales@wisdompubs.org • www.wisdompubs.org

the wisdom trust

As a not-for-profit publisher, Wisdom Publications is dedicated to the publication of fine Dharma books for the benefit of all and dependent upon the kindness and generosity of sponsors in order to do so. If you would like to make a donation to Wisdom, please do so through our Somerville office. If you would like to sponsor the publication of a book, please write or email us for more information.

Thank you.

Wisdom Publications is a nonprofit, charitable 501(c)(3) organization affiliated with the Foundation for the Preservation of the Mahayana Tradition (FPMT).